Data Demystified: A Beginner's Guide to Understanding the World Through Numbers

Ikwe Gideon

Published by Ikwe Gideon, 2024.

While every precaution has been taken in the preparation of this book, the publisher assumes no responsibility for errors or omissions, or for damages resulting from the use of the information contained herein.

DATA DEMYSTIFIED: A BEGINNER'S GUIDE TO UNDERSTANDING THE WORLD THROUGH NUMBERS

First edition. April 19, 2024.

Copyright © 2024 Ikwe Gideon.

Written by Ikwe Gideon.

Table of Contents

Data Demystified: A Beginner's Guide to Understanding the World Through Numbers 1

The Power of Data in the Modern World 4

Understanding Data 11

The Language of Data 19

Visualizing Data 29

Statistical Thinking 38

Data Collection and Management 53

Introduction to Data Analysis 66

Making Decisions With Data 79

Data in Business 93

Data in Healthcare 108

Data in Education 120

Data in Governance and Public Policy 132

Big Data and the Internet of Things (IoT) 143

Artificial Intelligence and Machine Learning 155

Protecting Your Data 167

Introduction

Have you ever wondered about the silent language that shapes our world? The one that predicts trends, influences decisions, and even dictates our personal preferences? Welcome to the realm of data, a domain where numbers narrate stories, trends forecast futures, and statistics hold the power to transform the abstract into the actionable. Imagine standing at the edge of a vast digital landscape, where every byte of information pulsates with potential. This is not the realm of the future; it is the vivid reality of our present, a reality where understanding data is no longer optional but essential. In a world awash with information, the ability to sift through noise to find the signal, to decode the complex into the comprehensible, is akin to possessing a superpower. But how does one begin to unravel the mysteries of data? How do we navigate this digital universe without getting lost in its infinite expanses? "Data Demystified: A Beginner's Guide to Understanding the World Through Numbers" embarks on this very quest. Through its pages, we journey from the ancient abacus to the quantum computing age, exploring how data has continually reshaped the human experience.

With every chapter, the book demystifies a piece of the vast puzzle, making the intricate dance of digits and datasets accessible to all. It's a journey that promises not just knowledge but empowerment. For in understanding data, we unlock new doors to innovation, equity, and sustainability. We learn not just to live in the digital age but to thrive in it, wielding data with precision and ethical consideration. As our exploration deepens, we encounter the guardians of this realm: privacy laws, ethical frameworks, and the unsung heroes of data governance. Their stories remind us that with great power comes great responsibility. Yet, as we stand on the brink of new discoveries in AI and machine learning, a question lingers, stirring the air like a whisper on the wind. A question that beckons you deeper into the heart of data, promising answers that could redefine our very understanding of the world. What if the key to unlocking the future lies not in the data we collect but in the questions we dare to ask?

In a realm where the silent language of data orchestrates the rhythm of our lives, one question echoes louder than the rest: What if the key to unlocking the future lies not in the data we collect but in the questions we dare to ask? This inquiry, both simple and profound, invites us on an odyssey—a journey not just through the landscape of numbers but into the very essence of our curiosity. It challenges us to look beyond the surface, to peel back the layers of the known and venture into the realm of possibility.

Let me share a story that illuminates the significance of our quest. Picture a bustling market in ancient Mesopotamia, the air thick with the aroma of spices and the murmur of a thousand conversations. Amidst this chaos, a merchant, with nothing but a primitive abacus and a keen sense of observation, uncovers patterns in trade that no one else sees. This ancient act of data analysis, rudimentary yet revolutionary, marks the dawn of our journey with data. It underscores a pivotal truth: our ability to understand and harness data has always been a cornerstone of human progress.

However, embarking on this journey is not without its perils. Misconceptions and challenges abound—obstacles that obscure our path and hinder our understanding. Many, caught in the whirlwind of big data and complex analytics, feel overwhelmed, viewing data as a domain reserved for the experts. Others, seduced by the sheer volume of information, mistake quantity for quality, chasing after data without discernment or direction.

The common response to this complexity is often a retreat to the familiar, a reliance on surface-level interpretations and oversimplified analyses. We see this in businesses that treat data as a mere byproduct of operations rather than as a strategic asset, in governments that lag in leveraging data for public good, and in individuals who navigate the digital world unaware of the data trails they leave behind.

Yet, the true solution lies not in retreat but in demystification. My approach, cultivated over decades at the intersection of data science and practical application, is to simplify without dumbing down, to illuminate without oversimplifying. "Data Demystified" is designed to be your compass in the

DATA DEMYSTIFIED: A BEGINNER'S GUIDE TO UNDERSTANDING THE WORLD THROUGH NUMBERS

digital wilderness, guiding you through the fundamentals of data, from its collection and analysis to its ethical use and beyond.

As you turn these pages, I invite you to forge a real connection with the world of data. Imagine yourself as a navigator, charting a course through the vast sea of information. With each chapter, you'll gain the tools and insights needed to interpret the digital signals that surround us, to make informed decisions, and to unlock new opportunities.

Envision the transformative power of data analytics in reshaping business strategies, in optimizing healthcare outcomes, in personalizing education, and in enhancing governance. Feel the thrill of discovery as you begin to see patterns where others see chaos, to find answers where questions abound.

And so, with a promise of enlightenment and empowerment, our journey begins. A journey that will not only demystify data but will also challenge you to view the world through the lens of curiosity and critical thinking. Through real-world applications, practical advice, and engaging storytelling, "Data Demystified" is more than a guide—it's a gateway to the future.

A future where data is not a barrier but a bridge, not a challenge but an opportunity. Where every individual, armed with knowledge and insight, can harness the power of data to navigate the complexities of the modern world. This is the promise of "Data Demystified: A Beginner's Guide to Understanding the World Through Numbers."

Welcome to the journey.

The Power of Data in the Modern World

Overview of Data's Significance

In the tapestry of human history, few threads are woven as intricately and as invisibly as that of data. From the earliest days of civilization, when tally marks on clay tablets recorded the yield of crops, to the present era, where vast digital landscapes are mapped out with billions of bytes, data has been the silent witness to our evolution. It has been our tool and our testament, a means to measure and a mirror to our progress. And yet, its significance often goes unnoticed, like the air we breathe, ever-present yet easily overlooked.

Why do we gather data? At its core, the collection of data is an expression of human curiosity, a desire to understand the world and our place within it. It is a quest for knowledge, driven by questions as simple as "how many?" and as complex as "why?". Data offers us the lens to bring the blurry edges of our understanding into sharp focus, to make informed decisions, and to foresee the impacts of those decisions on our future.

Consider the smartphone in your pocket or the laptop on your desk. These are not mere gadgets but portals to vast digital universes, each action and interaction generating data points that, when connected, reveal patterns and preferences. These devices empower us with information, yet they also make us contributors to the ever-expanding data cosmos. Every time we search the web, stream a video, or navigate with GPS, we are both consuming and creating data. It's a cycle as seamless as it is significant, highlighting the dual role we play in this digital age.

Data's impact transcends the personal, shaping industries and societies at a monumental scale. Take, for instance, the realm of healthcare, where data analysis has become a beacon of hope and innovation. Public health officials, armed with data, wage war against pandemics, tracing the spread of viruses, and predicting outbreaks before they occur. Here, data is not just numbers on a screen but lives saved, communities protected, and futures secured.

Similarly, the entertainment industry has been revolutionized by data, with streaming services like Netflix and Spotify using sophisticated algorithms to recommend shows and songs. These recommendations are not random but the result of meticulously analyzing viewing and listening habits, creating personalized experiences for millions of users. Such is the power of data to connect and to cater, transforming the way we consume media.

Yet, as we marvel at these advancements, we must also navigate the challenges that accompany them. The sheer volume of data generated daily can overwhelm, leading to analysis paralysis where decisions are delayed, and opportunities are missed. Moreover, the ethical use of data, particularly in protecting individual privacy, poses a persistent challenge, reminding us that with great power comes great responsibility.

How, then, do we harness this power responsibly? The answer lies in demystifying data, in understanding its nature, its nuances, and its potential. This book, "Data Demystified: A Beginner's Guide to Understanding the World Through Numbers," is your guide through this journey. It seeks not only to enlighten but to empower, equipping you with the knowledge to navigate the data-driven landscapes of our world.

In the chapters that follow, we will delve deeper into the mechanics of data collection, analysis, and interpretation. We will explore the ethical considerations essential for responsible data use and examine the role of data in driving innovation and fostering sustainable development. Through real-world examples, practical tips, and engaging narratives, this book will unravel the complexities of data, making it accessible and actionable for all.

Data shapes our decisions, from the mundane to the monumental. It informs our understanding of the world and our place within it. As we stand at the threshold of a future where data's influence only grows, let us embark on this journey of discovery with open minds and eager hearts.

Welcome to the world of data. Welcome to a journey of enlightenment. Welcome to "Data Demystified."

The Evolution of Data Usage

Embarking on this voyage through the annals of history, the evolution of data usage unfolds like an epic saga, where each chapter heralds new advancements, echoing the relentless march of human progress. From primitive tallying systems to the sophisticated digital algorithms that define our current era, data's journey mirrors the ascent of civilizations, showcasing a symbiotic relationship between societal advancement and the sophistication of data management techniques.

In the dim corridors of time, ancient civilizations laid the groundwork for data usage. Imagine the sun-drenched fields of Mesopotamia, where the first farmers marked clay tablets with simple lines, counting and recording the yield of their harvests. The invention of writing, a monumental leap forward, transformed data from transient whispers of oral tradition to enduring records. These early ledgers were not merely administrative tools but the harbingers of civilization itself, enabling the complex management of resources, the establishment of laws, and the birth of economies.

But why did ancient societies go to such lengths to record data? At its heart, the act of recording data was an assertion of control, a means to impose order on the chaos of the natural world. Through data, unpredictable floods became patterns to be anticipated, and bountiful harvests could be predicted and planned for.

Fast forward to the 17th century, a time when the winds of change were stirring once again. This era witnessed the birth of statistical analysis, a breakthrough that propelled data usage into new realms. In the hands of pioneers like John Graunt and Blaise Pascal, data began to reveal its true power, uncovering patterns and probabilities in the fabric of life itself. Graunt's analysis of London's mortality records laid the foundation for demography and epidemiology, turning data into a lens through which the health and dynamics of populations could be viewed.

Have you ever stopped to consider the profound impact of these advancements? The development of statistical analysis was revolutionary, enabling societies to not just record what had happened, but to anticipate what was to come. It was a shift from passive observation to active prediction, from merely navigating the river of time to steering its course with informed decisions.

The 20th century, with its wars and revolutions, brought about technological leaps that again transformed data usage. The invention of computers, those marvels of the modern era, marked a new dawn. Data, which had once been painstakingly inscribed on clay or painstakingly calculated with pen and paper, could now be processed at unprecedented speeds, stored in vast quantities, and analyzed with complex algorithms. This digital revolution did not just accelerate existing processes; it fundamentally altered the landscape of data usage, making what was once impossible commonplace.

Consider the explosion of digital data in the 21st century. In this digital age, we generate more data in a single day than was created in an entire year just a few decades ago. This deluge of data, from the vastness of the internet to the intimacy of wearable technology, offers unparalleled opportunities and challenges. The sheer scale of data today can be overwhelming, a boundless ocean of information. Yet, within this vastness lies the potential for profound insights into the human condition, from the mapping of human genomes to the prediction of global climate patterns.

The digital age has ushered in an era where data is not just an asset but a transformative force. Algorithms, those sets of rules for solving problems, now shape our world in profound ways, influencing everything from the news articles we see to the routes we take home. But as we stand on the brink of further breakthroughs, such as artificial intelligence and quantum computing, we must ponder a crucial question: how do we navigate this new world responsibly?

The journey of data is far from over. With each leap forward, new horizons of possibility open up, even as we grapple with the ethical implications of our newfound powers. The history of data usage is not just a record of human innovation; it is a mirror reflecting our collective ambitions, fears, and values.

So, as we chart the course of data's evolution, let us not forget the lessons of the past. Let us remember that data, in all its forms, is a tool forged by human hands, shaped by human minds, and wielded to shape our destiny. The future of data is not just a tale of technological triumph but a story of how we, as a society, choose to use this power.

In the chapters to come, we will explore the frontiers of data usage in the modern world, examining both the opportunities and the challenges that lie ahead. Together, we will demystify the complex algorithms that drive our digital age, unravel the ethical dilemmas posed by big data, and envision a future where data serves as a beacon of progress, illuminating the path toward a more informed, equitable, and sustainable world.

The story of data is the story of us. And it is a story that is still being written.

Objectives of the Book

In a world awash with numbers and statistics, understanding data is no longer a luxury but a necessity. "Data Demystified: A Beginner's Guide to Understanding the World Through Numbers" embarks on a mission to peel back the layers of complexity surrounding data, making it accessible to all. This book is not just a guide; it's a bridge connecting the layperson to the vast, often intimidating world of data analytics, statistics, and interpretation.

Why, one might ask, is such a journey necessary? The answer lies in the omnipresence of data in our daily lives. From the nutritional information on the back of a cereal box to the intricate algorithms that decide which advertisements you see online, data shapes our choices, opinions, and behaviors in countless ways. Yet, for many, data remains a distant, somewhat esoteric concept, appreciated only by statisticians and industry experts. This book aims to change that.

Our primary goal is to demystify data, to strip away the jargon and complexity that often shroud it in mystery. Imagine looking at a graph in the news and not just seeing lines and numbers, but understanding the stories they tell about economic trends, health statistics, or climate change. Picture yourself confidently navigating through misinformation, armed with the knowledge to question and critique the validity of the data presented to you. This book promises to equip you with that power.

Moreover, this guide seeks to instill a sense of confidence when encountering data in its various forms. Whether it's in personal decision-making, understanding public policies, or simply engaging in informed debates, a solid grasp of data empowers you to navigate the modern world more effectively. It's about transforming from a passive recipient of information into an active, discerning participant in the data-driven conversations that shape our society.

But our objectives extend beyond mere comprehension. In these pages, we delve into the ethical considerations surrounding data collection, analysis, and usage. With great power comes great responsibility, and the burgeoning capabilities of data analytics bring forth complex moral dilemmas. How do we protect individual privacy in the age of big data? What are the implications of algorithmic bias? By exploring these questions, we aim to foster a sense of ethical responsibility, encouraging readers to advocate for fairness, transparency, and accountability in data practices.

Furthermore, this book illuminates the potential of data to improve life. Beyond its applications in business and technology, data holds the promise to address some of the most pressing challenges facing humanity. From combating climate change to improving public health, data can be a force for good, driving innovation and fostering a more equitable society. Through real-world examples and case studies, we showcase the transformative power of data, inspiring readers to imagine how they, too, can contribute to positive change.

To achieve these objectives, "Data Demystified" employs a variety of strategies. Engaging narratives and vivid imagery bring abstract concepts to life, while direct questions invite reflection and personal connection. We limit the use of technical jargon, opting instead for clear, simple language that speaks directly to the reader. One-line paragraphs underscore key points, and a careful balance of rhythm and cadence ensures a pleasant reading experience. Throughout, quotations and dialogues add texture, offering insights from experts and laypersons alike.

In conclusion, this book is more than just a manual; it's a manifesto for a more data-literate society. It champions the belief that everyone, regardless of their background or profession, can appreciate the beauty and utility of data. By the end of this journey, readers will not only grasp the basics of data collection, analysis, and interpretation but will also appreciate the nuanced ethical debates and the immense potential that data holds to enrich our lives.

Data surrounds us, influences us, and tells the story of our world. With "Data Demystified," that story is yours to uncover, understand, and, ultimately, write.

Understanding Data

Defining the Building Blocks of Data

Imagine waking up to the gentle sound of rain tapping against your window. Instinctively, you decide to wear a raincoat and grab an umbrella before stepping out. Or consider the moment you peek into your refrigerator and notice you're out of milk, prompting a quick addition to your shopping list. What drives these decisions? Data. Unseen, yet omnipresent, data shapes our daily decisions, big and small. But what exactly is data? Let's demystify it together, revealing its essence through simple, everyday examples and diving deep into its various forms.

At its core, data is information. It's a collection of facts, measurements, or observations that can be analyzed to help us make informed decisions. Picture data as the lifeblood flowing through the veins of our decision-making processes, vital and transformative. From choosing what to wear based on the weather forecast to drafting a shopping list after an inventory check, data informs and guides our actions in myriad subtle ways.

But how do we categorize this omnipresent entity? Primarily, data splits into three broad types: structured, unstructured, and semi-structured. Each type, with its unique characteristics, plays a crucial role in the vast ecosystem of data processing and analysis.

Structured data, for instance, is the epitome of order and organization. Imagine a meticulously arranged bookshelf where each book is placed according to genre, author, or publication date. This ease of access and searchability mirrors the nature of structured data, typically stored in databases and spreadsheets. Its highly organized format allows for efficient processing and analysis, making it a cornerstone of traditional data management.

Visualize a spreadsheet listing every book in a library, with columns for titles, authors, genres, and publication years. This spreadsheet enables quick searches, such as all books published in the last decade or every novel by a specific author.

Structured data operates similarly, providing a clear, accessible framework for extracting specific information.

Unstructured data, on the other hand, is the wild, untamed counterpart to its structured sibling. Picture a vast, sprawling forest, each tree representing a piece of data – emails, social media posts, videos, and more. This data, in its rawest form, lacks the clear organization of structured data but holds a wealth of information waiting to be discovered. Navigating this forest requires more effort, as there's no predefined path to follow. Yet, the potential insights hidden within are boundless, offering rich, nuanced understanding of complex phenomena.

Consider the vast array of social media posts made every day. Each post, a tree in our metaphorical forest, may hold valuable insights into public opinion, emerging trends, or cultural shifts. Extracting and analyzing this information, however, presents a significant challenge due to the unstructured nature of the data.

Bridging the gap between structured and unstructured data, semi-structured data offers a blend of organization and flexibility. Imagine a garden where wildflowers grow alongside neatly arranged flower beds. This garden represents semi-structured data, like JSON or XML files, which, while not as rigidly structured as a database, include tags or markers to separate data elements. This semi-structured nature facilitates easier analysis than unstructured data while retaining more flexibility than structured data.

A JSON file storing information about books, for example, might include structured elements like title and author, alongside more flexible data such as reader reviews or related book suggestions. This blend of structure and flexibility makes semi-structured data a versatile tool in data analysis, capable of accommodating a wide range of information types.

Why does this matter? Understanding the different types of data and their characteristics empowers us to harness their potential more effectively. Whether making personal decisions based on weather forecasts and shopping lists or analyzing complex datasets to drive business strategy, recognizing the nuances of data types enhances our ability to interpret and act upon the information at our disposal.

Data, in all its forms, is the foundation upon which we build our understanding of the world. It guides our decisions, shapes our perceptions, and drives progress across every aspect of our lives. By demystifying data and exploring its building blocks, we equip ourselves with the knowledge to navigate the digital age more confidently and make informed decisions that shape our future.

As we continue on this journey of discovery, let's embrace the complexity and diversity of data, exploring its potential to transform our world. Data is not just numbers on a screen or words on a page; it's the key to unlocking the mysteries of the universe, one decision at a time.

Discovering Data Sources

In the previous chapter, we embarked on a journey, uncovering the essence of data and its types. Now, let's delve deeper, exploring the rich tapestry of sources from which this data springs. Like explorers discovering uncharted territories, we stand on the brink of understanding the myriad ways data enters our world.

At the heart of our exploration are two primary sources of data: manual and automated. Each offers a unique perspective, a different piece of the puzzle in our quest to understand the digital landscape.

Imagine stepping into the shoes of a researcher, clipboard in hand, ready to dive into the world of manual data collection. This method, though traditional, is far from outdated. Surveys, interviews, and observation - these are the tools of the trade, each with its own story to tell.

Surveys, with their structured questions, beckon for insights directly from the source - the people themselves. Picture a bustling city street, where every passerby holds a myriad of opinions, preferences, and experiences. Through surveys, we tap into this rich vein of information, gathering data that's as diverse as humanity itself.

Interviews, on the other hand, invite us into a more intimate space. Here, conversations unfold, revealing deeper insights that surveys might miss. Imagine sitting across from someone, delving into their thoughts and feelings, the ebb and flow of dialogue uncovering hidden gems of data.

Observation stands as the silent sentinel among manual methods. It requires no questions, no conversation. Instead, it watches, listens, and notes. Picture a researcher observing a marketplace, the interactions and transactions providing a wealth of data without a single word exchanged.

As we pivot from the manual to the automated, the scope of data sources expands exponentially. In this digital age, every click, every swipe, every online interaction leaves a trail - a digital footprint ripe for analysis.

Social media interactions, for instance, are a gold mine of data. Each like, share, and comment paints a picture of public opinion, trending topics, and social dynamics. Imagine the vast networks of connections, the billions of digital conversations happening at any moment. Here, in the virtual world, data flows freely, waiting to be captured and analyzed.

Online transactions offer another perspective. Every purchase, every booking, tells a story of consumer behavior, preferences, and trends. Picture the global marketplace, a web of digital storefronts where data on buying habits is just a click away.

But the realm of automated data collection doesn't stop at human interactions. The Internet of Things (IoT) has ushered in an era of devices that communicate, collecting and sharing data in real-time. From smart thermostats adjusting to our preferences to fitness trackers monitoring our health, IoT devices provide a continuous stream of data, offering insights into behaviors, habits, and trends.

Within this exploration of data sources lies the concept of Big Data - a term that evokes the vast, unbounded nature of the digital sea we navigate. But what exactly is Big Data? It's more than just volume; it's the variety, velocity, and veracity of data that characterize our digital world.

DATA DEMYSTIFIED: A BEGINNER'S GUIDE TO UNDERSTANDING THE WORLD THROUGH NUMBERS

Everyday activities, from browsing the internet to streaming videos, contribute to this colossal pool of data. Imagine the billions of data points generated daily, each a drop in the vast ocean of Big Data.

But why does this matter? Because within this ocean lies the potential for profound insights. Big Data, with its vast scope, offers a lens through which we can understand complex patterns, predict trends, and make informed decisions. It's not just about the amount of data, but what we do with it that counts.

At the forefront of this data revolution are IoT devices, the sentinels gathering information at the edge of our physical and digital worlds. These devices bridge the gap, turning the mundane into data points, the routine into insights.

Consider the simplicity of a smartwatch measuring our heartbeat or the complexity of a city-wide network of sensors monitoring traffic patterns. Each device, each sensor, contributes to a real-time understanding of the world.

It's a world where data is not static but dynamic, constantly evolving as it streams from countless sources. This real-time data offers a window into the now, allowing for immediate analysis and action. It's a game-changer, transforming how we understand and interact with the world around us.

As we traverse the landscape of data sources, from the manual to the automated, from individual interactions to the vast expanse of Big Data, we gain a deeper understanding of the digital ecosystem. It's a world where data is the currency, knowledge the reward.

But let us not forget, amidst this exploration, the human element. Data, in all its forms and sources, tells the story of us - our behaviors, our preferences, our world. It's a story that's constantly unfolding, one data point at a time.

As we continue on this journey of discovery, let us embrace the diversity of data sources, the potential of Big Data, and the insights offered by real-time data. For in understanding the world through numbers, we unlock the power to shape our future.

The Impact of Data Across Domains

In the mesmerizing journey of understanding data, we've traversed through the realms of its sources, types, and the groundbreaking concept of Big Data. Now, let's pivot our gaze to the horizon where the impact of data across various domains unveils a world transformed by numbers. This chapter, "The Impact of Data Across Domains," is designed to be your compass, guiding you through the intricate ways in which data reshapes industries, from healthcare and finance to education and beyond.

Imagine stepping into a hospital where every decision, from diagnosis to treatment, is underpinned by data. In healthcare, data is not just numbers; it's a beacon of hope, a lifeline that saves lives. Electronic health records (EHRs) provide a comprehensive view of a patient's history, enabling personalized care that was once a distant dream.

Picture a world where wearable devices monitor your vitals in real time, predicting health issues before they arise. With every heartbeat tracked, data becomes a guardian, offering a proactive approach to health rather than a reactive one. This transformation is palpable in the realm of research as well, where data analytics accelerates the discovery of breakthrough treatments and medications.

Now, let's navigate through the bustling streets of the financial district. Here, data is the currency of decision-making. Financial institutions leverage data to assess risk, tailor services, and predict market trends with astonishing precision.

Imagine investing in the stock market, guided by algorithms that analyze patterns and trends, minimizing risk while maximizing returns. In personal finance, data empowers individuals with insights into their spending habits, fostering financial literacy and smarter money management. This domain exemplifies how data, when harnessed wisely, can be a powerful engine for economic growth and stability.

Transitioning to the sphere of education, envision classrooms where learning is deeply personalized, catering to the unique needs and pace of each student. Data analytics in education paves the way for adaptive learning systems that

DATA DEMYSTIFIED: A BEGINNER'S GUIDE TO UNDERSTANDING THE WORLD THROUGH NUMBERS

identify areas of strength and weakness, customizing the curriculum accordingly.

This revolution extends beyond the classroom, offering educators insights into effective teaching strategies and student engagement. Data becomes a bridge, connecting educators, students, and parents in a collaborative effort to optimize learning outcomes. It's a world where education is no longer one-size-fits-all but a tailored journey that unlocks the full potential of every learner.

The impact of data stretches far and wide, touching every aspect of our lives. In transportation, data analytics optimizes routes, reducing traffic congestion and pollution. In agriculture, precision farming uses data to enhance crop yield and sustainability. The possibilities are boundless, limited only by our imagination and our willingness to explore.

Why is understanding these basics crucial? Because in a world awash with data, the ability to navigate this sea of information is a fundamental skill. It's about making informed decisions, fostering innovation, and solving complex problems.

As we stand at the crossroads of the digital age, the power of data beckons us to embark on a journey of discovery and transformation. It's a journey that requires curiosity, critical thinking, and a willingness to learn. But most importantly, it's a journey that promises to reshape our world, one data point at a time.

The journey through the impact of data across domains culminates in a realization: understanding data is not just an academic exercise; it's a stepping stone to thriving in a data-driven future. Whether in personal health, financial security, educational pursuits, or professional endeavors, data is a guiding light.

Let this chapter serve as a beacon, illuminating the path forward. Embrace the power of data, for it holds the key to unlocking a world of possibilities. As we delve deeper into this book, let's carry forward the insights gained, applying them to demystify the world through numbers.

In the grand tapestry of data, every thread, every color, every pattern is significant. Together, they weave a picture of a future where data is not just understood but harnessed to create a better, more informed world.

This is not the end but a new beginning in our journey to demystify data. Let's step into this future with confidence, armed with the knowledge that in the world of data, we are not mere spectators but active participants shaping our destiny.

The Language of Data

Decoding Data Terminology

Embarking on a journey through the complex yet fascinating world of data might seem daunting at first. However, understanding the language of data is akin to learning the alphabet before forming words—it's the foundation upon which everything else is built. So, let's dive into the essential terminology that serves as the bedrock of data understanding, shall we?

Imagine for a moment a library. This library, vast and varied, houses countless books covering every imaginable topic. Each book represents a dataset—a collection of related information neatly compiled for analysis. Just as a library organizes its books into sections, datasets are structured to facilitate understanding and exploration. They are the cornerstone of data analysis, offering a snapshot of information from which insights can be gleaned.

Now, think about what makes each book unique—it's the story, the characters, the themes, right? In the realm of data, these distinctive features are known as variables. Variables are the characteristics or attributes that we measure or observe; they're what make each data point unique. For instance, when considering a smartphone, variables might include its color, price, battery life, and screen size. Each variable offers a different perspective, a different lens through which we can understand the broader picture.

But how do we decide what to observe or measure? This is where the concepts of populations and samples come into play. Picture a forest teeming with wildlife. The entire forest represents a population—a complete set of items or individuals that share at least one characteristic. Studying every creature in the forest would be an insurmountable task. Instead, researchers might focus on a sample, a manageable subset of the population, like observing only the birds or a particular species of tree. Samples provide a practical means to draw conclusions about the larger population without the need to examine every single member.

At this juncture, you might wonder, "How do we ensure that our observations are accurate?" This question brings us to the notion of bias. Bias is the statistical skewing that can occur in data collection or analysis, leading to results that are systematically off the mark. It's like wearing tinted glasses that color your view of the world; what you see is not an accurate representation of reality. Recognizing and mitigating bias is crucial for drawing valid conclusions from data.

As we delve deeper, another term comes to the fore—correlation. Imagine two dancers moving in perfect harmony, their movements echoing each other. Correlation measures the relationship between two variables, indicating how likely they are to move together. However, it's vital to remember that correlation does not imply causation. Just because two variables appear to move in sync does not mean one causes the other to change. They might be dancing to the same tune, but it doesn't mean one is leading.

Consider now the power of visualization. A well-crafted chart or graph can illuminate relationships within data in a way that numbers alone cannot. Visualization transforms data into a visual context, making complex relationships more understandable. It's the difference between reading about a sunset and seeing one with your own eyes—the impact is immediate and profound.

In this digital age, another term has risen to prominence—big data. It refers to datasets so large and complex that traditional data processing tools cannot handle them. Imagine trying to listen to every conversation in a bustling city square; it's overwhelming. Big data requires advanced techniques to uncover patterns, trends, and associations, especially in human behavior and interactions.

Lastly, let's touch upon the concept of machine learning. Picture a child learning to ride a bike, gradually improving through trial and error. Machine learning algorithms do something similar with data—they learn from it, adapt, and make decisions or predictions based on that learning. It's a dynamic field that stands at the cutting edge of data analysis, continually evolving as more data becomes available.

In conclusion, the world of data is intricate and multifaceted, but it's built upon foundational concepts that are accessible with the right approach. By understanding these key terms—datasets, variables, samples, populations, bias, correlation, visualization, big data, and machine learning—we equip ourselves with the tools to unlock the stories hidden within data. And, like any skill, proficiency comes with practice and curiosity. So, let your curiosity lead the way as you continue to explore the vast, data-driven landscape that shapes our world.

Remember, data is not just numbers on a screen; it's a way to understand the pulse of humanity, the rhythms of nature, and the patterns that underpin our universe. With each term demystified, you're one step closer to deciphering the language of data, a language that holds the key to untold stories and insights waiting to be discovered.

Understanding Metrics and Variables

Delving into the realm of data further, we venture into a landscape shaped by metrics and variables. These elements are the tools with which we measure and understand the world in numbers, guiding us through the dense forest of information to clearings of insight and understanding. But what distinguishes a metric from a variable? How do they function in the grand tapestry of data analysis? Let's embark on a journey to demystify these concepts, making them as tangible as the objects in your home, as relatable as your daily experiences.

At the heart of our exploration are variables, the essence of diversity in the data world. Like the myriad of colors in a sunset, variables represent the different characteristics or quantities that we can measure or control. They are the individual threads that weave together to form the rich fabric of our analysis. But not all threads are the same. Variables split into two main categories: qualitative and quantitative.

Imagine you're attending a vibrant outdoor market. The cacophony of sounds, the kaleidoscope of colors, and the rich blend of aromas create a vivid sensory experience. Here, in this bustling environment, variables come alive. The qualitative variables are like the genres of music floating in the air—rock, jazz, classical—defying precise measurement but rich in descriptive quality. They tell us about the type or quality of an object or experience, akin to describing the mood of the market or the themes of the music.

In contrast, quantitative variables are the countable, measurable aspects. They are the number of market stalls, the price of a vintage record, or the weight of the fresh produce. These variables deal in numbers, providing a measurable dimension to our observations.

But where do metrics come into play? Metrics are the quantitative measures we use to assess, compare, and track performance or conditions. They are the compass by which businesses navigate their success, the heartbeat of progress. Consider a local coffee shop striving to measure its growth. Sales data, a quantitative variable, transforms into a metric of success as each transaction is recorded, analyzed, and compared over time.

Now, imagine the same coffee shop seeking to gauge customer satisfaction—an intangible, qualitative aspect. Through customer satisfaction surveys, qualitative variables like feedback comments are collected. Analyzing these responses, the coffee shop can derive metrics of customer happiness, translating abstract sentiments into actionable data.

Why is this distinction important? It guides our approach to data analysis, shaping the tools and methods we employ. A one-line answer cannot suffice the depth of this question, yet it beckons us to ponder the adaptability required in our analytical toolkit.

Consider the complexity of human behavior. How do we measure success, satisfaction, or even happiness? Through metrics and variables, we attempt to quantify the qualitative, to bring structure to the fluid dynamics of human experiences. This endeavor is not without challenges. As we translate the qualitative into quantitative measures, we navigate the delicate balance between accuracy and the essence of what we seek to measure.

Incorporating quotations from leading data scientists, one might find a common thread: "Data is a lens through which we view the world, a medium that captures the nuances of human experience in numbers and patterns." These words underscore the transformative power of data analysis, reminding us that behind every number, every metric, every variable, lies a story waiting to be told.

But how do we ensure these stories are not lost in translation? By engaging with data through the lens of metrics and variables, we adopt a language that bridges the gap between the tangible and intangible, the measurable and the descriptive. It is a language that demands both precision and creativity, a language that challenges us to look beyond the numbers and see the world anew.

In the narrative of data, metrics and variables are the protagonists, guiding us through a landscape rich with information and insight. They invite us to question, to explore, to understand the world through numbers. And as we journey through this landscape, we discover not just the power of data to inform and enlighten but also its capacity to connect us more deeply to the rhythms of life and the pulse of humanity.

So, as we close this chapter on metrics and variables, let us carry forward the curiosity and critical thinking that will illuminate our path through the vast, data-driven world. Remember, the journey of understanding data is not just about mastering the tools of analysis but about learning to see the world through the lens of numbers—a lens that reveals the hidden patterns, the unexpected correlations, and the stories that shape our understanding of reality.

In this journey, metrics and variables are our compass and map, guiding us through the complex terrain of data analysis. With them, we chart a course through the unknown, driven by the quest for knowledge and the thrill of discovery.

Exploring Data Dimensions

In our journey through the realm of data, we've acquainted ourselves with the vibrant mosaic created by metrics and variables. Like navigators of old, we've learned to chart our course using these tools, uncovering the stories whispered by numbers. Now, we turn our gaze to the horizon, where the concept of data dimensions awaits to further enrich our understanding. Imagine standing at the edge of a vast ocean, the expanse of data stretching out before you. Data dimensions are the means by which we can navigate these waters, offering a structured approach to understanding the complexity and richness of the information sea.

Data dimensions are akin to the fundamental coordinates that map our reality—latitude, longitude, and altitude—each adding a layer of depth to our understanding of the world. In the context of data, these dimensions can represent various attributes of information, such as time, location, and category. Each dimension adds a facet to our analysis, allowing us to dissect and comprehend the intricate patterns that would otherwise remain hidden in a flat sea of numbers.

Consider a simple example: a local bookstore tracking its sales. At a glance, sales figures over a month provide a snapshot of performance. Yet, this is a flat view, a single dimension of data. Now, introduce the dimension of time—daily sales figures across the month. Suddenly, patterns emerge; weekends show a sales spike, offering a richer insight into customer behavior.

But why stop there? Add another dimension—location. The bookstore operates in three different neighborhoods. Analyzing sales by location and time, it's revealed that the uptown branch outperforms the others on weekends. Is it the neighborhood demographics, the proximity to leisure spots, or perhaps the selection of books?

Now, incorporate the dimension of book categories—fiction, non-fiction, children's books. A vivid picture forms: on weekends, fiction sales soar at the uptown branch. The data now tells a story, not just of numbers, but of community preferences, of leisure habits, of cultural inclinations.

To visualize this, imagine a cube representing our sales data. The length of the cube could illustrate time, with each segment marking a day of the month. The width might represent different locations, each slice a different branch. The height could signify book categories, layer upon layer of genres. This cube, with its three-dimensional representation, allows us to dissect our sales data from

DATA DEMYSTIFIED: A BEGINNER'S GUIDE TO UNDERSTANDING THE WORLD THROUGH NUMBERS

multiple angles, offering a comprehensive understanding that was not possible when viewing data in a single dimension.

But the journey doesn't end here. The digital age introduces us to even more complex data structures. Social media analytics, for example, brings dimensions of sentiment, engagement rate, and viral reach. Each of these dimensions adds a layer, transforming our cube into a tesseract, a four-dimensional shape, challenging to visualize but rich in insights.

How, then, do we navigate this multidimensional data space? Visualization tools and data analytics platforms become our sextants and compasses, allowing us to chart a course through this complex information landscape. Simple bar graphs and pie charts evolve into heat maps, scatter plots, and multi-axis graphs, each tailored to explore the nuances of multidimensional data.

Imagine a dashboard where you can filter through dimensions, selecting different combinations to reveal hidden patterns or trends. Such tools empower us not just to view data but to interact with it, peeling back layers to uncover the stories beneath.

Why does this matter? In a world increasingly driven by data, understanding its dimensions is akin to learning a new language—a language that offers profound insights into customer behavior, market trends, social changes, and beyond. It's a language that enables businesses to make informed decisions, governments to tailor policies, and individuals to understand the world around them.

So, as we explore the dimensions of data, we embrace a more nuanced view of information. We learn not just to gather data, but to navigate its depths, discovering insights that guide us in our decisions, strategies, and understanding of the world.

Through the lens of data dimensions, we see not just numbers, but stories. Not just patterns, but possibilities. And as we continue our journey, let us remember: each dimension we add brings us closer to demystifying the vast, complex, and beautiful world of data.

In this exploration, remember, the power of data lies not in its volume, but in its structure, the dimensions we choose to explore, and the insights we glean from them. As we chart our course through the ever-expanding sea of data, let these dimensions be our guide, leading us to newfound understanding and discovery.

Practical Applications: From Theory to Action

Having voyaged through the theoretical underpinnings of data, we now stand on the threshold of practical application. This chapter, "Practical Applications: From Theory to Action," invites you on an expedition to apply your newfound knowledge in real-world scenarios. Let's transition from passive learners to active doers, turning abstract concepts into tangible skills.

Consider a hypothetical business scenario—Luna's Boutique, a burgeoning online fashion retailer. Luna's Boutique has been collecting data but is unsure how to utilize it effectively. Your mission, should you choose to accept it, involves identifying variables and metrics to help Luna's Boutique thrive.

First, identify the variables. Variables can be anything from the age of customers to the time spent on the website. For Luna's Boutique, key variables might include:

- Customer Age

- Purchase Frequency

- Average Spend per Visit

- Time on Site

- Product Views before Purchase

Each variable offers a glimpse into the customer journey, providing insights that can refine marketing strategies and enhance user experience.

Now, focus on the metrics. Metrics are the numerical values we assign to our variables to track performance over time. For our boutique, essential metrics could be:

DATA DEMYSTIFIED: A BEGINNER'S GUIDE TO UNDERSTANDING THE WORLD THROUGH NUMBERS

- Conversion Rate: The percentage of visitors who make a purchase.

- Customer Acquisition Cost: The total cost of acquiring a new customer.

- Lifetime Value: The total amount a customer is expected to spend in your boutique over their lifetime.

Armed with these variables and metrics, Luna's Boutique can begin to paint a clearer picture of their business health and customer behavior.

But let's delve deeper.

Imagine Luna's Boutique wants to increase its conversion rate. A simple dataset might include the number of website visitors, the number of purchases made, and the total revenue generated in a month. By analyzing this data, Luna's Boutique could identify patterns—perhaps most purchases are made late at night or after payday. This insight could lead to targeted promotions or sales during those peak times, potentially boosting the conversion rate.

To practice distinguishing between different types of data, consider the following exercise. Take the dataset mentioned above and categorize each piece of information. The number of website visitors and purchases made falls into quantitative data—data that can be measured and written down with numbers. Meanwhile, the type of products purchased is qualitative data—data that can be observed but not measured.

Now, let's apply what we've learned in a thought experiment. Imagine Luna's Boutique introduces a new line of eco-friendly apparel. How could they use data to assess the success of this line?

First, they could track the sales figures of the eco-friendly line compared to the non-eco-friendly lines. This is a direct quantitative comparison. Next, they might analyze customer feedback on the eco-friendly line, categorizing comments into positive, neutral, and negative. This qualitative analysis provides insights into customer sentiment.

But data analysis is not just about numbers and categories; it's about asking the right questions.

Why did sales of the eco-friendly line spike in the first month but then decline? Is there a correlation between positive customer feedback and repeat purchases? By constantly questioning and seeking answers through data, Luna's Boutique can make informed decisions that drive success.

As we wrap up this chapter, remember the journey from theory to action is ongoing. The world of data is dynamic, constantly evolving with the advent of new technologies and methodologies. The key to demystifying data lies not in mastering static knowledge but in cultivating a mindset of curiosity, flexibility, and relentless inquiry.

Data is a powerful tool, but its true value is unlocked only when applied with intention and insight. Like a map, it can guide us through the complexities of the modern world, revealing pathways to innovation, efficiency, and growth. As you close this book and embark on your own data-driven adventures, carry with you the lessons learned and the confidence to navigate the vast sea of information.

Remember, the journey of understanding the world through numbers is not just about reaching a destination. It's about the insights gained, the questions asked, and the mysteries uncovered along the way.

Dive deep into the data. Explore its dimensions. And let it illuminate the path to discovery.

Welcome to the world of practical data application. Your adventure begins now.

Visualizing Data

The Significance of Data Visualization

In the vast sea of numbers that is our world, data visualization emerges as a lighthouse, guiding us through the murky waters of complex information. Imagine, if you will, a dense forest of raw data. Without a map, navigating this forest would be an insurmountable challenge for many. Data visualization serves as that map, transforming the indecipherable into the understandable, the abstract into the concrete.

Why does this transformation hold such critical importance? Simply put, our brains are wired to process visual information far more efficiently than text or numbers. A well-crafted chart or graph can communicate trends, patterns, and outliers in a blink of an eye, which might take hours to decipher in a spreadsheet. Through the lens of visualization, data stops being just numbers on a page; it tells a story, evoking a more profound understanding and, ultimately, action.

Consider the historical example of John Snow's choleral outbreak map in 1854. At a time when the cause of cholera was unknown, Snow's innovative use of data visualization pinpointed the source of the outbreak to a single water pump on Broad Street in London. His map did not merely represent data points; it visualized a silent killer's path through the city, making the invisible visible. This breakthrough not only solved a deadly mystery but also laid the foundation for modern epidemiology. Snow's work underscores the power of visualization not just to inform but to change the course of history.

But how does one unlock this power? The key lies in understanding that data visualization is not merely about making data look appealing; it's about enhancing comprehension and insight. Effective visualizations strip away the superfluous, highlighting what matters most. They invite the viewer to explore, discover, and, most crucially, to question. What trends emerge from this graph? Why does this outlier exist? These questions pave the way for deeper analysis and informed decision-making.

Indeed, the art and science of data visualization have evolved. Tools and technologies have advanced, enabling more complex data to be visualized in increasingly innovative ways. Interactive dashboards, real-time data maps, and immersive 3D models are just the tip of the iceberg. Yet, the fundamental goal remains the same: to illuminate the truth hidden within the data.

Now, one might wonder, how does one begin to navigate the vast landscape of data visualization? The journey starts with simplicity. A compelling visualization needs no embellishment. Its power lies in its ability to convey complex information straightforwardly and intuitively. This principle guides the choice of colors, shapes, and layouts - each element serving a purpose, each detail enhancing clarity.

The matter of selecting the right type of visualization cannot be overstated. Pie charts, bar graphs, scatter plots - each has its unique strengths and best use cases. A pie chart, for instance, excels in showing parts of a whole, while a scatter plot can reveal correlations between variables. The decision should be driven by the data's story and the insights one wishes to highlight.

Equally important is the ethical dimension of data visualization. Misleading representations can distort the truth as much as they can reveal it. Thus, integrity in visualization design is paramount. This means avoiding manipulative practices like cherry-picking data or using misleading scales. The objective is to inform, not deceive.

In the realm of data visualization, less is often more.

A single, well-designed chart can speak volumes, transforming raw data into a compelling narrative. This narrative has the power to inform policies, drive business strategies, inform research, and spark social change. It makes the invisible visible, the incomprehensible understandable.

In conclusion, data visualization stands as a beacon in our data-driven age, a tool of immense power and potential. It bridges the gap between data and decision-making, between information and action. As we venture further into this age, the ability to visualize data effectively will not just be a skill but a necessity. The journey through the dense forest of data is fraught with challenges, but with visualization as our map, we are well-equipped to navigate it.

And so, we must ask ourselves: What stories lie hidden in the data awaiting to be told? What discoveries await on the horizon of visualization?

The answers, like the data itself, are limitless.

Tools and Techniques for Visual Representation

Embarking on the journey of data visualization requires a compass to navigate the diverse array of tools and techniques available. This chapter serves as that compass, guiding you through the landscape of visual representation, from the simplest charts to the most intricate visualizations. Understanding these tools is akin to learning a new language—a language that speaks through shapes, colors, and patterns to convey the rich stories hidden within data.

Visualize, for a moment, a bar chart. Its simplicity belies its power. Each bar, varying in height, stands as a testament to a piece of the data's story. Why choose a bar chart? For its unparalleled ability to compare quantities across different categories. Whether assessing sales figures across different regions or evaluating voter turnout in successive elections, bar charts transform numerical data into immediate visual comparisons. Their strength lies in their clarity and directness, making them an ideal starting point for beginners.

Imagine a line graph's smooth curve, rising and falling like the contours of a landscape. Line graphs excel in depicting trends over time, allowing the observer to trace the arc of a story as it unfolds across days, months, or years. They invite the viewer on a journey, revealing patterns such as seasonal fluctuations in temperature or the gradual growth of a startup. By connecting data points with lines, they highlight the continuous flow of data, making them indispensable for analyzing time series data.

Consider the humble pie chart, a circle divided into slices, each representing a proportion of the whole. Despite debate over its effectiveness, the pie chart shines when illustrating simple part-to-whole relationships in datasets with a limited number of categories. A single glance can reveal, for instance, the market share of different companies or the distribution of spending in a household budget. However, wield pie charts with caution; they can quickly become confusing when overloaded with slices.

Heat maps use color gradients to represent variations in data, creating a tapestry of hues that can unveil patterns and correlations at a glance. From spotting high crime areas in cities to identifying popular times for gym attendance, heat maps synthesize complex data into an intuitive visual form. Their beauty lies in their ability to make the density of data palpable, turning numbers into a symphony of colors that speaks directly to our visual intuition.

When exploring relationships between two variables, scatter plots emerge as a powerful ally. Each point on a scatter plot represents a data pair, with its position determined by the values of the two variables. These plots are adept at revealing correlations, trends, and outliers, making them invaluable in fields ranging from economics to health sciences. A well-crafted scatter plot can, for instance, expose the relationship between advertising spend and sales revenue, guiding strategic decisions.

How, then, does one select the appropriate visualization technique? Begin by asking: What story does the data tell? What insights am I seeking to uncover? The answers will steer you towards the visualization method that best aligns with your objectives. Remember, the goal is not merely to display data but to illuminate it.

Fortunately, for those embarking on their data visualization journey, an array of user-friendly software and online platforms stands ready to assist. Tools like Tableau, Microsoft Power BI, and Google Data Studio offer robust capabilities for creating dynamic visualizations, even for those with little to no coding experience. Meanwhile, platforms such as D3.js cater to those willing to delve into the coding aspect, offering unparalleled flexibility and power.

A single, well-chosen visualization can illuminate the hidden narrative within vast datasets, transforming abstract numbers into insights and actions. As we continue to navigate the era of big data, the ability to effectively visualize information is not just a skill but a vital literacy.

So, what story will your data tell? Which visualization will you choose to bring that story to life? The journey of data visualization is not just about presenting data; it's about revealing the truth, sparking curiosity, and inspiring action. Armed with the tools and techniques outlined in this chapter, you are now better equipped to embark on this journey, to explore the world through numbers, and to tell the stories that matter.

As we move forward, let us remember: In the realm of data visualization, every chart, every graph, every map is a window into the heart of our data-driven world. The possibilities are as boundless as the data itself.

Design Principles for Effective Visualizations

In the quest to transform raw data into compelling visual stories, the principles of effective visualization design play a pivotal role. These principles, including simplicity, clarity, accuracy, and consistency, serve as the scaffolding upon which all informative and engaging visualizations are built. Choosing the right visual format for the data and audience, utilizing color and layout with intention, and steering clear of common pitfalls are all critical steps in crafting visualizations that not only inform but also inspire.

Simplicity, the first of these principles, cannot be overstated. A cluttered visualization overwhelms the viewer, obscuring the data's story rather than illuminating it. Consider a complex graph brimming with unnecessary decorative elements. Now, imagine stripping away those elements until only the essential data remains. The transformation can be startling. A clean, uncluttered visualization emerges, allowing the viewer's eye to focus on what truly matters—the data.

Clarity follows simplicity. A visualization should convey its message with unmistakable precision. To achieve this, every element, from typography to axis labeling, must be selected for maximum legibility and understanding. Misleading axes or unclear labels can quickly lead to misinterpretation. Hence, clarity ensures that the viewer grasps the intended message without ambiguity.

Accuracy in data visualization is the cornerstone of trust. Even the most aesthetically pleasing graph loses its value if the data it represents is inaccurately portrayed. This calls for meticulous attention to detail in how data scales are represented and how data points are plotted. An accurate visualization respects the data's integrity, presenting it without distortion or manipulation.

Consistency in design aids in comprehension across multiple visualizations. By maintaining uniform styles, colors, and formats, viewers can quickly orient themselves when moving from one visualization to another. This principle is particularly vital in reports or presentations containing multiple graphics. Consistency acts as a visual language, guiding the viewer through the data narrative with ease.

The selection of the right visual format hinges on the data's nature and the story it tells. Does the data show a trend over time? A line graph might be most effective. Is the goal to compare quantities? Perhaps a bar chart is the answer. The key is to match the visualization format with the data's story, ensuring that the chosen format amplifies the message rather than muddling it.

Effective use of color and layout can dramatically enhance a visualization's impact. Color, when used judiciously, can draw attention to key data points, differentiate categories, and guide the viewer's eye through the data journey. However, an overreliance on color or poor color choices can lead to confusion or misinterpretation. Similarly, a thoughtful layout organizes elements in a way that feels natural to the viewer, making the data's story unfold logically and intuitively.

Avoiding common pitfalls is crucial for effective visualizations. Among these pitfalls are overcomplication, lack of focus, and misleading representations. An overcomplicated visualization tries to say too much at once, scattering the viewer's attention. A visualization lacking focus has no clear message, leaving viewers puzzled about its purpose. Misleading representations, whether intentional or not, distort the viewer's understanding of the data, eroding trust and credibility.

To breathe life into these principles, let's examine a before-and-after scenario. Imagine a bar chart intended to show sales figures across regions. The original version uses a dizzying array of colors, 3D bars, and a cluttered background. The revised version adopts a flat design, uses a consistent color scheme to differentiate regions, and employs a clean background. The result? A visualization that communicates its message clearly, accurately, and effectively.

In your journey of data visualization, never underestimate the power of small changes. A shift in color, a simplification of design, or a clearer label can transform a confusing graph into an insightful story. Remember, the goal is not merely to show data but to reveal its narrative in a way that engages, informs, and inspires.

As we continue to explore the vast landscape of data visualization, these design principles serve as our compass. They guide us in creating visualizations that not only stand out for their aesthetic appeal but, more importantly, for their ability to communicate complex information with simplicity and precision.

Now, the question beckons: How will you apply these principles to your next visualization project? Will you choose simplicity over complexity, clarity over confusion? The decisions you make will shape the stories your data tells, leaving a lasting impression on your audience.

In the realm of data visualization, every choice matters. Let these principles light your way, and may your visualizations illuminate the world of data like never before.

Data Storytelling: Beyond Charts and Graphs

Data storytelling transcends the realm of mere charts and graphs. It invites the audience into a narrative, weaving numbers and facts into a compelling tale that resonates on a personal level. This chapter delves into the art and science of data storytelling, illustrating how to transform dry statistics into engaging stories that captivate and educate. Through vivid examples and practical advice, we'll explore the power of narrative in making data come alive.

Imagine a world where numbers speak as eloquently as words, where data sets become characters in a story, each with its own journey and destination. This is the essence of data storytelling. It's not just about presenting data; it's about telling a story that connects on an emotional level, making complex information accessible and memorable.

To begin, consider the story behind the data. Every dataset has a narrative arc waiting to be uncovered. Start by asking, "What is the story here?" Is it a tale of growth, a saga of struggle, or an account of unexpected discovery? Identifying the narrative thread is the first step in crafting your story.

Next, understand your audience. Who are they? What do they know, and what do they need to know? Tailoring your story to your audience ensures that it resonates and provides value. Whether you're addressing policy makers, business leaders, or the general public, the goal is to make your audience care about the data as much as you do.

Now, let's weave the narrative. Effective data storytelling often follows a classic structure: introduction, development, climax, and conclusion. Begin by setting the scene, introducing the data and its context. Develop the story by exploring the data, highlighting trends, patterns, and anomalies. Lead your audience to the climax, the pivotal moment where the data reveals its most significant insights. Finally, conclude by reflecting on the implications of the data, calling your audience to action or leaving them with a thought-provoking question.

Visualizations play a crucial role in data storytelling, but they should serve the narrative, not dominate it. Choose visualizations that support and enhance the story, making complex data understandable at a glance. Remember, simplicity and clarity are your allies. A well-chosen chart can illuminate a trend or highlight a key point, but a cluttered or confusing visualization can obscure the story you're trying to tell.

Consider the power of personalization. Incorporating personal stories or testimonials can add a human dimension to your data, making abstract numbers feel concrete and relatable. When people see themselves reflected in the data, they're more likely to engage with the story and absorb its message.

DATA DEMYSTIFIED: A BEGINNER'S GUIDE TO UNDERSTANDING THE WORLD THROUGH NUMBERS

Now, let's look at some real-world examples of data storytelling in action:

1. In the fight against smoking, public health organizations have used data storytelling to powerful effect. By presenting data on smoking's health impacts alongside personal stories of affected individuals, they've crafted compelling narratives that have spurred action and policy change.

2. Climate change activists use data storytelling to communicate the urgency of their cause. By combining data visualizations showing rising temperatures and melting ice caps with stories of communities and species at risk, they create an emotional connection that motivates people to act.

3. Companies use data storytelling to inform strategy and drive decisions. For example, a retailer might use data on shopping patterns to tell a story of changing consumer behavior, guiding the development of new products or marketing strategies.

In conclusion, data storytelling is a powerful tool for making sense of the world through numbers. By combining narrative elements with data visualizations, we can tell stories that engage, inform, and inspire. Whether you're seeking to influence policy, drive business decisions, or simply broaden your audience's understanding, remember that behind every dataset is a story waiting to be told.

And now, a question for you: What stories will you tell with your data?

Let this be your guiding principle as you venture beyond charts and graphs, into the rich and transformative world of data storytelling.

Statistical Thinking

Embracing a Statistical Mindset

In today's information-saturated world, the ability to sift through data, discern patterns, and make informed decisions is not just an asset—it's a necessity. This necessity underscores the importance of adopting a statistical mindset. But what does it truly mean to think statistically? At its core, statistical thinking enables us to navigate the sea of numbers, charts, and graphs that inundate our daily lives, transforming raw data into meaningful insights. It's about seeing beyond the numbers, understanding the stories they tell, and making sense of the world in a quantitatively informed way.

Imagine, for a moment, you're a meteorologist tasked with predicting tomorrow's weather. With a statistical mindset, you don't just consider the temperature readings of the past week. Instead, you analyze patterns over years, considering variability, trends, and anomalies. This approach offers a more nuanced forecast, one that accounts for the unexpected. Similarly, a business owner forecasting next quarter's sales dives deep into historical data, identifies seasonal trends, and adjusts for market conditions. These examples underline a fundamental truth: Statistical thinking illuminates the path from data to decision, highlighting risks, uncertainties, and opportunities.

Why, though, do many find the leap to statistical thinking challenging? Often, it's because numbers can intimidate, appearing as cold, hard facts that resist interpretation. Yet, embracing a statistical mindset is akin to learning a new language—the language of data. Like any language, fluency comes with practice, patience, and, importantly, a willingness to immerse oneself in the culture of numbers.

Consider the variability inherent in any dataset. Variability tells us that no two data points are exactly alike, and this diversity holds the key to understanding the bigger picture. By acknowledging and analyzing variability, we unlock the stories data wants to tell us. Whether it's the fluctuation in your daily step

DATA DEMYSTIFIED: A BEGINNER'S GUIDE TO UNDERSTANDING THE WORLD THROUGH NUMBERS

count or the variation in weekly sales at your local cafe, each deviation from the average is a piece of the puzzle.

Uncertainty, too, plays a crucial role in statistical thinking. To embrace uncertainty is to acknowledge that our predictions about the future are educated guesses, influenced by the quality and quantity of data we have. It's a humbling realization, but one that sharpens our decision-making, guiding us to consider a range of outcomes rather than a single, definitive answer.

But how does one begin to cultivate a statistical mindset? Start with curiosity. Ask questions. Why did sales spike last month? What factors contribute to a successful product launch? From there, dive into the data, seeking patterns and anomalies. Employ visual tools like graphs and charts to bring data to life, making it easier to spot trends.

Remember, statistical thinking is not about performing complex calculations or using sophisticated software (though these skills are valuable). It's about asking the right questions, considering the context, and being mindful of the limitations of your data.

Let's take a simple example to illustrate this point. Say you notice a correlation between the number of hours spent studying and exam scores among students. A statistical mindset prompts you to consider other factors that might influence this relationship. Are students who study more also getting more sleep? Do they have access to better study materials? By considering these questions, you move beyond surface-level observations, delving into the complex web of factors that influence outcomes.

This approach to data is not just for scientists or business analysts. It's for everyone. From making personal finance decisions to understanding public health information, a statistical mindset empowers you to make choices based on evidence, not just intuition or hearsay.

Embrace uncertainty. Welcome variability. Dive deep into the data, and let it guide you to informed, nuanced decisions. This is the essence of a statistical mindset. It's a journey worth taking, one that enriches your understanding of the world and enhances your ability to navigate it.

In conclusion, adopting a statistical mindset is akin to putting on a new pair of glasses. Suddenly, the world looks different. Patterns emerge from what once seemed like random noise. Risks and opportunities become clearer. Decisions feel grounded in evidence, not just guesswork.

Embracing a statistical mindset is not just about becoming better at handling data. It's about becoming a more informed citizen, a more astute professional, and, ultimately, a more engaged human being. As you continue on this journey, remember: the world of data is vast, but it's also incredibly fascinating. Let your curiosity guide you, and you'll find that numbers have much to teach us about the world—and about ourselves.

Basic Statistical Concepts

Embarking on the journey to demystify data, we now turn our gaze to the foundational stones of statistical analysis. These are not mere stepping stones but the bedrock upon which the edifice of understanding stands. At the heart of this exploration lie concepts so fundamental, yet so profound, that they shape our very approach to data: populations and samples, random sampling, and the concept of distribution.

Imagine, if you will, a vast ocean. This ocean, teeming with life, represents a population. In the context of statistics, a population encompasses the entirety of entities under study. It could be every customer of a multinational corporation, every star in the galaxy, or every grain of sand on a beach. The sheer scale of a population can be awe-inspiring, yet analyzing every single member of this vast group is often impractical, if not impossible.

Here, the concept of a sample comes into play. A sample is akin to a single drop of water from our metaphorical ocean. Though minuscule in comparison to the ocean, this drop can tell us volumes about the characteristics of the entire body of water, provided it is representative. Drawing a sample means selecting a portion of the population to analyze, in hopes of gaining insights into the larger whole. Consider the company seeking to understand its customers' satisfaction. Surveying every customer could be a Herculean task. Thus, a sample, a manageable yet representative group, becomes the focus.

DATA DEMYSTIFIED: A BEGINNER'S GUIDE TO UNDERSTANDING THE WORLD THROUGH NUMBERS

But how does one ensure that this sample accurately reflects the population? Enter random sampling, a method as critical as it is elegant. Random sampling involves selecting members of the population in such a way that every individual has an equal chance of being chosen. This randomness is crucial; it wards off bias, allowing the sample to mirror the population's diversity truly. Picture a vast field of flowers, each a different hue. Random sampling is the blindfolded selection of blooms that, together, represent the field's colorful tapestry.

Now, with a representative sample in hand, we turn to another cornerstone of statistics: the concept of distribution. Distributions describe how values in a dataset are spread out or dispersed. They are the patterns we discern in the data, the shapes that emerge when we chart our findings. To understand distribution is to grasp the range and tendency of data, to see beyond individual numbers to the story they collectively narrate.

One of the most common and illuminating distributions is the bell curve, or normal distribution. It resembles, as the name suggests, a bell, with most data points clustering around the mean in the center and fewer values trailing off toward the extremes. This pattern reveals the natural tendency of many phenomena to hover around an average, with outliers on either end. It's a concept that resonates deeply with the human experience, reflecting the variability and patterns inherent in nature and society.

Why, though, does this matter? Why delve into populations and samples, wrestle with randomness, and ponder distributions? The answer is simple yet profound. These concepts are the lenses through which we view data, the tools by which we extract meaning from the morass of numbers. They empower us to make inferences about a population based on a sample, to generalize findings and draw conclusions that transcend the data at hand.

Consider the implications for a moment. A well-chosen sample can illuminate trends in customer behavior, predict electoral outcomes, or gauge public opinion on pressing issues. Through the prism of statistical concepts, raw data transforms into actionable insights, guiding decisions in business, policy, and everyday life.

Yet, this is but the beginning. As we peel back the layers of data, more complex and nuanced concepts await. But the journey through the basics—populations and samples, random sampling, and distribution—lays the groundwork for deeper exploration. It is a testament to the power of statistics to not only inform but also inspire.

In the realm of data, numbers are not mere figures; they are the language of the universe, whispering the secrets of the world. As we continue our journey through the pages of this book, let us carry forward the lessons learned, the curiosity kindled, and the insights gleaned. For in the quest to demystify data, every concept mastered is a step closer to understanding the world through the eloquent language of numbers.

And so, we advance, armed with the knowledge of basic statistical concepts, ready to delve deeper into the mysteries of data. The path ahead is rich with discovery, promising revelations that will further our journey from data to decision, from uncertainty to understanding.

Welcome to the world of statistics, a realm where numbers narrate tales, patterns predict possibilities, and data divulges its depths. Together, let us unravel the stories woven into the fabric of data, for in these tales lies the power to illuminate the world.

Measures of Central Tendency and Variability

Venturing further into the heart of statistical analysis, we embark on a journey to understand the essence of data through its most telling descriptors: measures of central tendency and measures of variability. These tools not only summarize a dataset succinctly but also unveil the underlying stories numbers whisper about trends, behaviors, and anomalies.

At the core of our exploration are the measures of central tendency: mean, median, and mode. Each serves as a beacon, illuminating the central point around which data points rally.

The mean, or the average, emerges as the first of these guiding lights. Calculating it involves summing all values in a dataset and dividing by the

DATA DEMYSTIFIED: A BEGINNER'S GUIDE TO UNDERSTANDING THE WORLD THROUGH NUMBERS

number of observations. Imagine a classroom where students have just received their math test scores. Adding all scores and dividing by the number of students yields the average score, offering a glimpse into the overall performance. Yet, the mean is sensitive to outliers — those scores dramatically higher or lower than the rest. A single extraordinary score can skew the mean, drawing it towards the outlier.

Then, there's the median, the middle value when all observations are ordered from least to greatest. Picture a line of people, arranged by height. The person standing precisely in the middle represents the median height, unaffected by the towering basketball player at one end or the child at the other. This resilience to outliers makes the median a robust measure of central tendency, particularly useful in skewed distributions.

The mode, the most frequently occurring value in a dataset, offers another perspective. Consider a shoe store's sales data. If a particular shoe size sells out faster than others, it becomes the mode, pointing to the most popular size. Unlike the mean and median, the mode can handle categorical data, such as shoe sizes or color preferences, providing insights into the most common category.

Transitioning from the center to the spread of data, we delve into measures of variability: range, variance, and standard deviation. These metrics illuminate the diversity within a dataset, revealing the extent of variation from the average.

The range, the simplest of these measures, calculates the distance between the highest and lowest values. A classroom's test scores, ranging from 50 to 100, suggest a wide disparity in performance. However, the range overlooks the distribution of scores between these extremes, offering a limited view of variability.

More nuanced is the variance, which measures the average squared deviation from the mean. It quantifies the spread of data points, providing a comprehensive view of variability. Yet, its squared units can be perplexing, distancing the measure from the actual data.

Enter the standard deviation, the square root of variance, which returns to the original units of the data. It signifies the average distance of data points from the mean, offering a digestible measure of dispersion. A small standard deviation indicates tight clustering around the mean, while a larger value suggests widespread data points.

Why, though, do these measures matter? In the realm of data, understanding both the central tendency and variability is crucial. Together, they paint a fuller picture of a dataset, guiding decisions and predictions. For instance, a business analyzing customer spending patterns would find the mean spending valuable. Yet, knowing the standard deviation of this spending reveals the consistency of customer behavior, essential for tailoring marketing strategies.

Consider a practical dataset: the heights of a group of individuals. Calculating the mean height provides a summary, but incorporating the standard deviation uncovers the diversity within the group. Such insights could prove invaluable in designing products or services tailored to this group's needs.

Through vivid examples and straightforward calculations, we've ventured deep into the heart of data analysis, uncovering the essence of datasets through their central tendencies and variabilities. These measures, though simple at first glance, are powerful tools in interpreting the world through numbers.

As we continue this journey, remember: behind every dataset lies a story waiting to be told. Through the lenses of mean, median, mode, range, variance, and standard deviation, we gain the clarity to understand these narratives, guiding our decisions and shaping our perceptions of the world.

In the chapters that follow, we'll build upon this foundation, exploring more complex statistical tools and techniques. Yet, the lessons gleaned here will remain central, for they are the keystones of statistical analysis, the means by which we transform raw data into meaningful insights.

And so, armed with these tools, let us press forward, ever curious, ever learning, on our quest to demystify data. For in the numbers that define our world, there lies a wealth of knowledge, awaiting those with the courage to seek it.

Welcome to the next chapter in understanding the world through numbers.

Understanding Distributions

Embarking on the next leg of our data analysis voyage, we dive into the realm of distributions, a concept that not only enriches our understanding of data but also forms the backbone of many statistical methodologies. Distributions offer a way to visualize and understand how data points are spread or distributed across different values. Imagine entering a vast garden where each flower represents a data point. The way these flowers spread across the garden, clustering in some areas and scattering in others, tells you about the garden's distribution of flora.

Among the pantheon of distributions, the normal distribution reigns supreme, often heralded as the bell curve for its symmetrical, bell-shaped appearance. Why does this particular distribution hold such a pivotal place in the realm of statistics? The answer lies in its ubiquity and the fundamental role it plays in the central limit theorem, which suggests that, given a large enough sample size, the distribution of the sample means will approximate a normal distribution, regardless of the original data's distribution.

Visualizing a normal distribution, one can't help but notice its beautifully balanced shape, where the mean, median, and mode coincide at the center. This symmetry means that data points are equally likely to fall on either side of the mean, diminishing in frequency as they move further away. The spread of a normal distribution is determined by its standard deviation, a measure that reveals how tightly data points cluster around the mean.

Why is this structure so crucial? Many psychological and physical measurements (e.g., IQ scores, heights) follow a normal distribution, making it an indispensable tool in social sciences, natural sciences, and engineering. It provides a foundation for inferential statistics, enabling us to make predictions and decisions about populations based on sample data.

Let's delve deeper into the significance of understanding distributions by considering a manufacturer concerned with quality control. This company could use a normal distribution to predict the variation in the dimensions of produced parts. Parts that fall within a specific range around the mean dimension are acceptable, whereas those that lie in the tails of the distribution may be too large or too small, leading to defects. By understanding the distribution of these dimensions, the manufacturer can minimize waste and improve product quality.

But not all data fits neatly into a bell curve. Some distributions skew left or right, stretching the tail longer on one side. Skewed distributions are particularly telling. A right-skewed distribution, where the tail extends more to the right, indicates that a significant number of observations are larger than the mode. Conversely, a left-skewed distribution suggests the opposite. These nuances can dramatically affect decision-making and interpretation of data. For instance, in education, exam scores that skew left might indicate a test that was too difficult for most students, prompting educators to adjust their teaching strategies.

Picturing these distributions can be as simple as plotting data points on a graph or as sophisticated as employing software tools that render complex statistical visualizations. These visual aids are not merely academic; they are practical tools that guide decision-making in fields as diverse as finance, healthcare, and public policy.

Consider a graph displaying the distribution of exam scores in a large class. At a glance, an educator can see whether the scores cluster around a high, medium, or low average and whether any outliers may indicate cheating or scoring errors. This immediate visual assessment can inform whether the curriculum needs adjustment or if additional support is necessary for students.

Why stop at normal and skewed distributions? The statistical universe teems with other types, each suited to specific kinds of data and analysis. For example, the uniform distribution, where every outcome has an equal chance of occurring, is ideal for simulating random events like lottery draws. Meanwhile, the exponential distribution helps model the time between independent events that occur at a constant average rate, essential in fields like network theory and survival analysis.

In a world increasingly driven by data, understanding distributions is akin to mastering a language. It enables us to interpret the world's complexity through the lens of probability, making sense of randomness and variability. Through distributions, we gain insights into patterns and trends that inform decisions, shape policies, and ultimately, help us navigate the uncertain terrain of the future.

So, as you stand at the threshold of this new chapter, remember: distributions are not just mathematical constructs. They are the keys to unlocking the stories data tells us about the world. With this knowledge, you are better equipped to make informed decisions, whether you're assessing risk, analyzing market trends, or simply trying to understand the natural phenomena that shape our lives.

Armed with this deeper understanding of distributions, especially the paramount normal distribution, we are now poised to explore more complex statistical territories. Yet, no matter how far we venture, the fundamental insights gleaned from distributions will remain our guiding stars, illuminating the path toward data enlightenment.

The Role of Probability in Statistics

In the captivating journey of unraveling the mysteries of data through statistics, we now embark on a path less trodden but equally fascinating—the role of probability in statistics. This chapter aims to demystify the concept of probability, a cornerstone of statistical analysis, and illustrate its profound significance in interpreting the world around us through numbers.

Understanding the essence of probability is akin to acquiring a new lens through which we view reality. At its core, probability measures the likelihood of an event occurring. But what does this mean in the context of our daily lives? Imagine you're about to pull a marble from a bag filled with marbles of different colors. The chance of drawing a red marble, for instance, depends on the number of red marbles in the bag relative to the total number of marbles. This scenario, simple yet powerful, encapsulates the essence of probability.

Let's delve deeper.

Probability ranges from 0 to 1, where 0 indicates impossibility and 1 ensures certainty. But the world we inhabit thrives on the nuances that lie between these extremes. Consider the weather. What does a 70% chance of rain mean? It suggests that, based on historical data and current conditions, rain has occurred 70 out of 100 times under similar circumstances. Here, probability bridges our understanding of the past with predictions about the future.

But how do we harness probability in statistics to make such predictions? At the heart of this endeavor is the concept of random variables and probability distributions. A random variable assigns a numerical value to each possible outcome of a random process. For instance, when flipping a coin, we might assign a 0 to tails and a 1 to heads. The probability distribution, then, is a map that assigns a probability to each possible outcome of our random variable.

Pause for a moment.

Reflect on the beauty of this system. It provides a structured way to quantify uncertainty, offering a glimpse into the likely outcomes of phenomena that seem governed by chance.

In applying probability to real-world data, statisticians often rely on specific probability distributions, each suited to particular types of data or events. The binomial distribution, for example, models the number of successes in a fixed number of independent trials, each with the same probability of success. This distribution could apply to a wide range of situations, from guessing the number of heads in a series of coin flips to predicting the success rate of a new marketing campaign.

One might wonder, however, about the practicality of probability in everyday decision-making. The answer lies in the realm of inferential statistics, where probability forms the backbone of hypothesis testing and confidence intervals. Through these tools, we can make informed guesses about population parameters based on sample data, gauging the reliability of our estimates.

Imagine, for instance, a pharmaceutical company testing a new drug. By using probability, researchers can determine the likelihood that the observed effects of the drug are due to chance. This process involves calculating a p-value, a probability that measures the evidence against a null hypothesis. A low p-value suggests that the observed data is unlikely under the null hypothesis, thereby providing evidence in favor of the alternative hypothesis.

This example underscores a pivotal point: probability empowers us to make decisions in the face of uncertainty. Whether in medicine, business, or public policy, the ability to assess risks and make predictions based on incomplete information is invaluable.

Yet, the beauty of probability lies not only in its applications but also in its philosophical implications. It challenges our perceptions of randomness and determinism, prompting us to ponder the very nature of chance. Is the universe inherently random, or does it follow deterministic laws that we have yet to fully understand? Probability invites us to explore these questions, offering a mathematical framework that mirrors the complexity of the world around us.

As we conclude this chapter, it's clear that the role of probability in statistics is both foundational and transformative. By providing the tools to quantify uncertainty, probability enables us to make sense of data, draw conclusions, and predict future events with a measure of confidence. Through its applications, we gain insights into the probabilities that shape our decisions, our policies, and, ultimately, our understanding of reality.

Dive into the next chapter with this newfound appreciation for probability, ready to explore how it intertwines with other statistical concepts to unlock the stories hidden within data. Embrace the journey ahead, for it is through the lens of probability that we begin to see the world not as a series of coincidences but as a tapestry woven from the threads of chance and certainty.

Statistical Thinking in Everyday Life

Statistical thinking, though often cloaked in the mantle of academia and professional jargon, permeates our daily lives, influencing decisions both mundane and monumental. As we journey further into the realm of understanding our world through numbers, it becomes increasingly clear how integral statistical thinking is to navigating the complexities of everyday life. This chapter aims to demystify the process of applying statistical concepts to our personal and professional scenarios, encouraging a more informed, critical approach to decision-making and problem-solving.

Imagine standing at the crossroads of a major life decision – perhaps choosing a new career path, investing in real estate, or deciding on a medical treatment. Each path ahead is shrouded in uncertainty, with potential risks and benefits lurking in the shadows. Here, statistical thinking illuminates the way, helping us evaluate our options not on gut feeling alone but on solid, empirical evidence.

Consider the simple act of reading the news. Headlines bombard us with percentages, averages, and trends, each clamoring for our belief and acceptance. Yet, without a critical eye trained through statistical thinking, we risk being swayed by misleading or misinterpreted data. How often have we encountered sensational claims that, upon closer examination, crumble under the weight of statistical scrutiny? Developing a habit of questioning the source, the sample size, and the context of data presented in the media transforms us from passive consumers of information to active, discerning analysts.

Engaging with statistics in our professional lives opens yet another avenue for applying these critical skills. In the fast-paced world of business, understanding consumer behavior trends through statistical analysis can be the difference between soaring success and catastrophic failure. By dissecting data on customer preferences, purchase patterns, and market dynamics, businesses can make strategic decisions that are grounded in reality rather than conjecture.

But how does one cultivate this statistical mindset? Start by embracing curiosity. Question the numbers and the conclusions drawn from them. Dive deeper into the methodology behind the statistics you encounter. Was the sample size adequate? Were the variables controlled appropriately? What assumptions underpin the analysis? By dissecting the data process, you not only sharpen your critical thinking skills but also become more adept at identifying reliable information.

DATA DEMYSTIFIED: A BEGINNER'S GUIDE TO UNDERSTANDING THE WORLD THROUGH NUMBERS

Another key strategy is to practice. Like any skill, statistical thinking becomes more intuitive with use. Analyze the statistics you encounter in your daily life, from the effectiveness of a new diet to the reliability of a car brand based on customer satisfaction surveys. With each analysis, the process of questioning, understanding, and applying statistical concepts will become more fluid.

But beware the pitfalls of statistical thinking. Avoid becoming so ensnared in the quest for data that you overlook the human element. Numbers tell a story, but they are not the entire narrative. Remember to consider the ethical, social, and personal implications of the data you encounter. Statistics are a tool, not a dictator of decisions.

Consider this scenario: You're evaluating health risks associated with various lifestyle choices. The statistics indicate a correlation between certain behaviors and increased health risks. Armed with this information, you're better positioned to make informed choices about your lifestyle. However, it's essential to remember that correlation does not imply causation. Just because two factors are related statistically doesn't mean one causes the other. This critical distinction underscores the importance of not just understanding statistics but interpreting them wisely.

As we conclude this exploration into the utility of statistical thinking in everyday life, let's reaffirm our commitment to becoming more critically minded, analytical consumers of information. By applying the principles of statistical thinking to our daily decisions, we not only empower ourselves with a deeper understanding of the world but also foster a more rational, evidence-based approach to problem-solving.

In a world increasingly driven by data, the ability to navigate the sea of numbers with confidence and insight is more valuable than ever. Let the journey into statistical thinking not intimidate but inspire you. For in the mastery of statistics lies the key to unlocking a world of informed decisions, reduced uncertainty, and enhanced understanding. Embrace the challenge, for the rewards are manifold and profound.

Your journey through the world of data and statistics does not end here. Let each day be an opportunity to apply, question, and expand your statistical knowledge. As you move forward, carry with you the critical thinking skills honed through this exploration. For it is through the lens of statistical thinking that you will find clarity in complexity, making informed decisions that enrich both your personal and professional life.

Remember, the power of statistics is not just in the numbers but in the stories they tell and the decisions they inform. Welcome to a world demystified, where the beauty of data unfolds before you, guiding your path through the numbers.

Data Collection and Management

Strategies for Effective Data Collection

Embarking on a journey into the vast universe of data collection, one quickly realizes the landscape is as diverse as it is intricate. With myriad methods at our disposal, from the traditional pen-and-paper surveys to the cutting-edge digital tools, the quest to gather valuable information might seem daunting at first glance. Yet, understanding these varied strategies, their merits and pitfalls, is akin to holding a map in the realm of numbers and trends.

Surveys, for instance, stand as time-honored sentinels of data collection. Through carefully crafted questions, they probe the minds of respondents, offering insights that are both broad in scope and rich in detail. Imagine a survey as a canvas, where each response adds a stroke of color, gradually revealing a masterpiece of public opinion or customer satisfaction. However, designing this canvas demands meticulous attention to avoid leading questions or ambiguity that could cloud the clarity of the data.

Interviews, on the other hand, delve deeper, offering a more nuanced palette of information. They are the magnifying glass through which we can explore the contours of human experience, one story at a time. Yet, the beauty of this method lies not just in the depth of insight but also in the rapport between interviewer and interviewee, a dance of words that can illuminate hidden truths. The drawback? Subjectivity and the substantial investment of time and resources.

In the digital age, web scraping emerges as a modern marvel, tirelessly sifting through the Internet's vast expanses to harvest data. Like miners extracting precious ores, these tools uncover trends, patterns, and insights from the digital terrain. The allure of automation and efficiency is undeniable, but so are the ethical quandaries and the specter of data privacy concerns that loom large.

Similarly, the Internet of Things (IoT) sensors are the silent observers, meticulously recording every fluctuation in their environment. From the rhythm of a city's heartbeat to the subtle changes in a vineyard's microclimate, these devices capture the essence of their surroundings. The challenge here lies in the sheer volume of data generated and the technical prowess required to distill meaningful insights from this ocean of information.

How does one navigate this labyrinth of options? The key lies in clarity of purpose. What are the whispers you're trying to hear in the cacophony of data? Are you seeking broad trends or intimate stories? The answer to these questions will be your North Star, guiding you to the appropriate method.

Quality and integrity of data, however, are the bedrock upon which all analysis stands. Imagine building a house on sand; without a solid foundation, even the most magnificent structure crumbles. Similarly, data collected without regard for accuracy, privacy, and ethical considerations is like a mirage, enticing but ultimately devoid of substance.

Designing effective surveys, therefore, is not merely an exercise in question formulation but a commitment to fairness and transparency. It is about crafting a bridge of trust between you and the respondent, ensuring that each question is a step towards mutual understanding rather than a leap into bias.

Ethics, too, cannot be an afterthought. In a world increasingly scrutinized for privacy breaches and data misuse, ethical data collection is not just a legal requirement but a moral imperative. It is a pledge to treat every piece of information with the respect it deserves, recognizing that behind every data point is a human story.

In conclusion, the art of data collection is a delicate balance between science and empathy, technology and ethics. As you embark on this journey, let curiosity be your compass, integrity your anchor, and respect for privacy your guiding light. Remember, the goal is not just to gather data, but to illuminate the shadows, revealing insights that can transform our understanding of the world.

So, dear reader, as you stand at the threshold of this adventure, ask yourself: what stories do you wish to uncover? What truths lie hidden, waiting to be brought to light? The answers await, in the numbers, in the patterns, in the silent whispers of data.

Organizing and Storing Your Data

In the previous chapter, we embarked on a journey through the intricate realm of data collection, a foundational step in understanding the whispers and roars of the world through numbers. Now, let's pivot to an equally crucial aspect: organizing and storing this data. Imagine a treasure trove of precious stones, each representing a piece of data. Without a system to categorize and secure these gems, their value diminishes, lost in the chaos. This chapter is your map to prevent such disarray, guiding you through the caverns of data organization and storage.

Organizing Your Data: The First Step to Clarity

Before delving into the specifics of data storage, let's address the initial task at hand: organization. Why, you might wonder, is this step so critical? Consider a library with thousands of books haphazardly scattered. Finding a specific title in this mess would be akin to searching for a needle in a haystack. Similarly, data, when improperly organized, can become overwhelming, rendering it nearly impossible to extract meaningful insights.

Databases and spreadsheets stand as the sentinels of data organization. A database, with its structured format, is akin to a well-organized library, where information is stored in tables, akin to bookshelves, making retrieval a breeze. Spreadsheets, on the other hand, offer a canvas for smaller datasets, allowing for easy manipulation and analysis.

Moreover, data management software emerges as a powerful ally, offering tools to categorize, edit, and visualize data, transforming raw numbers into comprehensible insights. Imagine wielding a magic wand that organizes books in a library with a flick, categorizing them by genre, author, or any parameter of choice. This is the prowess of modern data management tools.

Basics of Data Storage for Beginners

As you journey further into the world of data, understanding the basics of data storage becomes imperative. At its core, data storage serves as the digital equivalent of a vault, safeguarding information for future retrieval and analysis. This vault can exist in various forms, each with its unique characteristics.

Types of Data Storage

The landscape of data storage is vast, featuring primary types such as Hard Disk Drives (HDDs), Solid State Drives (SSDs), and cloud storage. HDDs, akin to vast warehouses, offer ample space at a lower cost, making them ideal for storing large volumes of data. However, they can be slower and more prone to physical damage.

SSDs, in contrast, are like sportscars - sleek, fast, and efficient. They access data at lightning speeds, providing a significant performance boost, albeit at a higher cost.

Then there's cloud storage, a concept that has revolutionized data management. Imagine entrusting your precious stones to a master jeweler, who keeps them secure and accessible whenever needed. This is the essence of cloud storage - data is stored on the internet, maintained by a provider, ensuring accessibility from anywhere in the world.

Introduction to Cloud Storage

The allure of cloud storage lies not just in its accessibility but in its scalability. As your treasure trove grows, cloud storage adapts, offering more space without the need for physical upgrades. This flexibility, combined with the cost-effectiveness of paying only for the space you need, makes cloud storage an attractive option for many.

Data Storage and Security Basics

However, with great power comes great responsibility. The security of your stored data cannot be overstated. Encryption and strong passwords act as formidable gates, deterring unauthorized access. Furthermore, the practice of backing up data ensures that, even in the face of disaster, your information remains safe.

Imagine encrypting a book in a library, making its contents readable only to those with the key. This is the essence of encryption in data security - a shield guarding your digital treasures.

Considerations for Choosing a Storage Solution

Choosing the right storage solution is akin to selecting the perfect home for your treasures. Consider factors such as the amount of data, the necessity for quick access, and budget constraints. Each storage option comes with its set of advantages and limitations; understanding your needs is the first step towards making an informed decision.

Looking Forward: The Future of Data Storage

As we stand on the brink of technological advancements, the future of data storage promises innovations that could further simplify and secure data management. From advancements in SSD technology to breakthroughs in cloud storage, the landscape is ever-evolving.

One-line paragraph for emphasis:

The journey of data, from collection to storage, is a testament to the power of organization and the importance of security.

By unraveling the complexities of data storage and organization, this chapter serves not just as a guide but as a beacon, illuminating the path for beginners. As you delve into the realm of data, remember, the key to unlocking its potential lies in understanding how to store and organize it effectively. Let this knowledge be the foundation upon which you build your expertise, exploring the world through the lens of numbers with confidence and curiosity.

Protecting Data: Security and Privacy Considerations

Embarking on the journey of data organization and storage brings us to the critical crossroads of security and privacy considerations. An unseen but ever-present threat looms over the digital treasures we've so meticulously sorted and stored. In this chapter, we delve deep into the fortress of data protection, armed with the tools and knowledge to shield our assets from prying eyes and malicious intents.

The Shield of Encryption

Imagine a diary, its contents brimming with the most intimate thoughts and secrets. Without a lock, its pages are vulnerable to any curious eye. Encryption acts as that lock for digital data, converting information into an unreadable format for anyone who does not possess the key. This process ensures that even if data falls into the wrong hands, its confidentiality remains intact.

Encryption does not stand alone; it is part of a broader strategy to protect data both at rest and in transit. For data on the move, protocols like SSL (Secure Sockets Layer) and TLS (Transport Layer Security) create secure channels, preventing unauthorized interception. How does this work in practice? Consider sending a letter through a securely locked tube system, accessible only to the sender and the intended recipient. This is the essence of encrypted data transmission - a direct, secure pathway shielded from external threats.

The Art of Anonymization

Anonymization strips data of personal identifiers, transforming it into a state where individuals cannot be identified. This technique is particularly crucial when dealing with sensitive information in fields such as healthcare or finance. Through processes like data masking and pseudonymization, personal details are obscured, rendering the data useful for analysis while protecting individual privacy.

Why is this significant? Imagine a mosaic artwork, each piece representing a snippet of personal data. Anonymization is like rearranging the pieces so that the original image - the identifiable person - can no longer be discerned. This method safeguards privacy while allowing valuable insights to be gleaned from the data.

Secure Data Sharing Practices

DATA DEMYSTIFIED: A BEGINNER'S GUIDE TO UNDERSTANDING THE WORLD THROUGH NUMBERS

Sharing data is often necessary, whether for collaborative projects, compliance with legal requirements, or for the purpose of innovation. However, sharing does not mean compromising security. Secure data sharing practices include the use of secure file transfer protocols, access controls, and the principle of least privilege, ensuring that individuals have access only to the data necessary for their role.

Consider a bank vault where each employee has a key. Not all keys open every lock; instead, each key grants access only to specific areas. This analogy illustrates the principle of least privilege in action - a cornerstone of secure data sharing that minimizes the risk of data exposure.

Navigating the Legal Landscape

The legal and ethical landscape of data handling is a labyrinth of regulations designed to protect personal and sensitive information. Laws such as the General Data Protection Regulation (GDPR) in the European Union and the Health Insurance Portability and Accountability Act (HIPAA) in the United States set stringent guidelines for data privacy and security.

Compliance with these regulations is not merely a legal obligation but a testament to an organization's commitment to protecting individual rights. Failure to comply can result in severe consequences, including hefty fines and irreparable damage to reputation. Thus, understanding and adhering to these laws is paramount for any entity handling data.

Lessons from the Frontlines: Case Studies of Data Breaches

History is rife with tales of data breaches, each a cautionary tale underscoring the importance of robust security measures. Consider the breach of a major retail corporation, where millions of customers' credit card information was compromised. Or the cyberattack on a healthcare provider, resulting in the unauthorized access of patient records. These incidents are not merely stories of loss and violation but pivotal learning opportunities.

Each case study reveals common vulnerabilities, such as inadequate encryption, weak passwords, or the lack of a comprehensive security strategy. They also illuminate the path forward, highlighting the effectiveness of proactive measures like regular security audits, employee training on phishing awareness, and the implementation of advanced threat detection systems.

The consequences of neglecting data security are stark, serving as a clarion call for vigilance and action.

Conclusion: A Call to Arms

As we navigate the digital age, the responsibility to protect data is a mantle we must all bear. From encryption to anonymization, secure data sharing practices, and compliance with legal regulations, the tools at our disposal are both varied and powerful.

But remember, the landscape of data security is ever-evolving, with new threats emerging as quickly as the technologies developed to counter them. Staying informed, vigilant, and proactive is not just advisable; it is essential.

In this chapter, we've traversed the complex terrain of data security and privacy, uncovering the strategies and practices that form the bedrock of data protection. As we move forward, let's carry these lessons with us, guarding our digital treasures against the threats that lurk in the shadows.

After all, in the world of data, vigilance is not just a strategy—it's a necessity.

Ensuring Data Quality and Integrity

In the vast expanse of the digital age, data serves as the compass by which we navigate. Quality and integrity are the twin beacons that guide this journey, ensuring that every piece of information we rely on is both accurate and reliable. But how do we maintain these critical standards amidst the ever-growing sea of data? The answer lies in a comprehensive approach to data management, where validation, cleaning, and regular auditing become part of our navigational charts.

The Pillars of Data Quality

DATA DEMYSTIFIED: A BEGINNER'S GUIDE TO UNDERSTANDING THE WORLD THROUGH NUMBERS

Imagine entering a library in search of wisdom, only to find the books filled with inaccuracies and falsehoods. Such is the peril of compromised data quality. To avoid this, we must first understand the pillars that uphold the sanctity of data: completeness, consistency, accuracy, relevance, and timeliness. Each of these attributes plays a vital role in ensuring that data serves its intended purpose, much like the ingredients of a masterful recipe that combine to create a culinary masterpiece.

The Art of Data Validation

Data validation acts as the gatekeeper, ensuring that only data which meets our predefined standards enters our systems. This process begins with the crafting of rigorous criteria, tailored to the specific needs of each dataset. For instance, consider a database designed to track the migration patterns of monarch butterflies. The validation rules for this database might include checks for geographical coordinates within a certain range, ensuring that each entry is both relevant and accurate.

Why is this meticulous approach necessary? Incorrect data can lead to misguided conclusions, much like a misread map can send a traveler down the wrong path. Through validation, we safeguard the integrity of our data, ensuring that our analyses and decisions are built on a solid foundation.

The Crucial Task of Data Cleaning

Even with stringent validation, some erroneous data will inevitably slip through. Data cleaning is our method of rectifying these inaccuracies, a process akin to weeding a garden to allow the true beauty of the flowers to shine. This task involves identifying and correcting (or removing) inaccuracies, duplicates, and inconsistencies within our datasets.

One might question, "Is this process truly necessary?" The answer is a resounding yes. Clean data is the lifeblood of accurate analysis, enabling us to draw insights and make decisions with confidence. It ensures that our data reflects the reality it seeks to represent, untainted by errors or anomalies.

The Role of Regular Auditing

Data is not a static entity; it evolves and grows over time. Regular auditing acts as a health check, ensuring that our data management practices continue to meet the high standards of quality and integrity we have set. This involves reviewing the entire lifecycle of our data, from collection and storage to its eventual use.

Consider the practice of auditing akin to a yearly physical examination. Just as we seek to identify potential health issues before they become serious, auditing allows us to spot weaknesses in our data management practices early on, ensuring that our data remains robust and reliable.

Governing Data with Precision

At the heart of our efforts to ensure data quality and integrity lies the establishment of robust data governance policies. These policies define the standards and procedures for data management, serving as the rulebook by which we play the game. Within this framework, the role of a data steward becomes paramount. This individual, or team, is charged with overseeing data quality and compliance, ensuring that the rules of the game are followed.

Why is governance so crucial? Without these guiding principles, our data management efforts can become disjointed and ineffective. Data governance provides the structure needed to navigate the complexities of data management, ensuring that each step taken is in service to the overarching goal of maintaining data quality and integrity.

Data Stewardship: The Guardians of Quality

The data steward acts as the guardian of data quality, wielding the tools of validation, cleaning, and auditing with precision and care. Their mission is to ensure that data management practices not only adhere to established standards but also evolve in response to new challenges and opportunities.

Imagine a vigilant caretaker of a vast and varied garden, who knows every plant and understands the nuances of its care. Just as this caretaker ensures the health and beauty of the garden, the data steward ensures the quality and integrity of our data, guiding it safely through its lifecycle.

Conclusion: A Commitment to Excellence

In the realm of data, quality and integrity are not mere aspirations; they are necessities. Through the meticulous practices of data validation, cleaning, and auditing, guided by robust governance policies and the careful oversight of data stewards, we can ensure that our data remains a reliable compass by which we navigate the world.

Let us, then, commit to these principles of data management, for in this commitment lies the key to unlocking the true potential of our digital age. In ensuring the quality and integrity of our data, we pave the way for insights and innovations that can transform our understanding of the world.

After all, in the universe of data, maintaining quality and integrity is not just a practice—it's a promise.

Data Management Tools and Technologies

In the labyrinth of the digital age, data management tools and technologies emerge as the torchbearers, illuminating the path toward insightful decision-making and strategic insights. As we delve deeper into the realm of data, understanding the myriad of tools at our disposal becomes not just beneficial but essential. This chapter aims to demystify the wide spectrum of data management technologies, guiding you through the selection of the right tools based on the unique dimensions of your data needs.

Embarking on this journey, we start with the fundamentals: spreadsheet applications. Picture a humble artist beginning with a simple palette of colors. In much the same way, spreadsheet software like Microsoft Excel or Google Sheets offers a foundational platform for data management. These tools, with their grid-like interface, allow for the organization, analysis, and storage of data in a structured format. Their versatility shines in smaller projects or for individuals taking their initial steps into data management. Features such as formula-based calculations, pivot tables, and basic data visualization tools make spreadsheets an indispensable ally in the data management arsenal.

Yet, as our data aspirations grow, so too does the complexity of our tools. Enter database management systems (DBMS), the heavy lifters of the data world. Imagine constructing a skyscraper. Just as architects and engineers require more sophisticated materials and tools, managing larger and more complex datasets demands robust solutions like MySQL, Oracle, or PostgreSQL. These systems allow for efficient data storage, retrieval, and manipulation through the use of structured query language (SQL), offering a powerful way to interact with large volumes of data. The key lies in understanding the nature of your data and the goals you aim to achieve. Questions like "How vast is my dataset?" or "What level of data complexity am I dealing with?" can guide you in selecting a DBMS that best fits your needs.

But what happens when your data outgrows the confines of traditional databases? This is where data warehouses and data lakes enter the scene, serving as repositories capable of storing massive volumes of structured and unstructured data. Imagine a vast ocean (data lake) teeming with all manner of marine life (data), from structured swarms of fish (traditional row-based data) to the unstructured majesty of whales (videos, images, etc.). In contrast, a data warehouse can be likened to a curated aquarium, where only selected species are housed, representing structured, processed data ready for analysis. Tools like Amazon Redshift for data warehousing and Apache Hadoop for data lakes offer scalable and flexible solutions to manage the deluge of data faced by organizations today.

The march of progress in data management also brings cloud storage solutions to the forefront, offering a nimble and scalable alternative to on-premise storage. Services like Amazon S3, Google Cloud Storage, and Microsoft Azure Blob Storage provide secure, accessible, and cost-effective options for storing vast amounts of data. The cloud's allure lies not just in its storage capabilities but in the seamless integration with analytics and machine learning services, unlocking the full potential of your data.

As we navigate the vast seas of data, the compass of our journey must be calibrated to the specific requirements of our data endeavors. Features such as scalability, reliability, security, and ease of use stand as beacons guiding our

DATA DEMYSTIFIED: A BEGINNER'S GUIDE TO UNDERSTANDING THE WORLD THROUGH NUMBERS

selection of data management tools and technologies. It's not about wielding the most advanced tool; it's about mastering the right tool for the task at hand.

In the quest to tame the wilds of data, one truth remains constant: the landscape of data management tools and technologies is ever-evolving. Staying informed and adaptable, willing to learn and experiment with new solutions, ensures that your data management practices remain not only effective but transformative.

Imagine standing atop a mountain, surveying the horizon. Each tool, each technology, represents a path through the wilderness of data. Choosing your path wisely, armed with the knowledge and understanding of what each tool offers, you can navigate the complexities of data management with confidence.

In the end, data management is not just about managing numbers; it's about unlocking the stories those numbers tell, the insights they reveal, and the decisions they inform. It's about understanding the world through the lens of data. And with the right tools in hand, the possibilities are limitless.

Introduction to Data Analysis

The Essence of Data Analysis

Data whispers secrets about the universe, secrets that only keen ears can decipher. Imagine a world where decisions, big and small, are not left to chance but are crafted with precision and foresight. This is the domain of data analysis, a realm where numbers and figures transform into insights and strategies. At its core, data analysis involves a meticulous process of inspecting, cleansing, transforming, and modeling data. The aim? To unearth valuable information, draw meaningful conclusions, and bolster decision-making processes. The implications of this are vast and varied, touching every corner of the modern world.

Consider the entrepreneur, grappling with the future of a fledgling product. Through the lens of data analysis, customer feedback becomes a goldmine of insights, guiding refinements and enhancements. Or picture a healthcare professional, analyzing patient data to tailor treatments that promise better outcomes. These scenarios are but a glimpse into the transformative power of data analysis.

Why is this process so pivotal across different domains? The answer lies in its ability to convert raw data into actionable intelligence. Data analysis can unveil patterns and trends that might otherwise remain obscured. This can lead to strategic advantages that are both significant and sustainable.

Take, for instance, the realm of retail. A simple analysis of sales data can reveal the most popular products, the times of year when sales peak, and the customer demographics most likely to make a purchase. Armed with this knowledge, a retailer can make informed decisions about inventory, marketing strategies, and even store layouts.

But how does one embark on this journey of discovery? It begins with the cleansing of data, a crucial step that ensures accuracy by removing any errors or inconsistencies. Next comes the transformation of data, where it is organized or

DATA DEMYSTIFIED: A BEGINNER'S GUIDE TO UNDERSTANDING THE WORLD THROUGH NUMBERS

structured in a way that makes analysis possible. Finally, modeling data involves using statistical methods to predict outcomes or understand relationships.

Let's delve deeper. Imagine a bakery that decides to analyze its sales data. The owner notices that sales of chocolate chip cookies spike on rainy days. Intriguing, isn't it? This insight leads to a strategic decision to increase the production of chocolate chip cookies on weather forecasted to be rainy. The result? Happier customers and a noticeable uptick in sales.

Why does this matter? Because in an age where information is abundant, the ability to sift through noise and find the signal is invaluable. It's about making informed decisions rather than relying on intuition alone.

But it's not just about business or healthcare. Data analysis has the power to address societal challenges, from managing natural resources more efficiently to understanding the impacts of policy changes on communities. The potential is limitless.

Consider this: every piece of data has a story to tell, if only we're willing to listen.

But how can one ensure that the story is not just heard but understood? By embracing simplicity. In a discipline as complex as data analysis, the temptation to delve into technical jargon is ever-present. Yet, the true mastery of data analysis lies in making the complex accessible. It's about painting a picture with numbers, using vivid imagery and relatable examples to bring data to life.

Imagine standing at the edge of a serene lake, throwing a pebble, and watching the ripples spread. Each ripple represents an insight gained from data analysis, spreading knowledge and understanding across the surface of decision-making.

Occasionally, a question breaks the silence: "What if we looked at the data differently?" This simple query can lead to breakthroughs, challenging assumptions and encouraging exploration.

Data analysis is a journey, not a destination. It's about continuously asking questions, seeking answers, and being open to new possibilities.

In a world awash with data, the ability to analyze and interpret this data is a superpower. It's what turns challenges into opportunities, questions into answers, and data into decisions.

This, dear reader, is the essence of data analysis.

Unlocking the secrets whispered by data requires patience, curiosity, and a willingness to venture into the unknown. It's a journey that promises not just insights, but transformation.

Embrace it.

Data Analysis Process: A Step-by-Step Guide

Embarking on the journey of data analysis is akin to setting sail into a vast ocean of information. The horizon stretches far and wide, filled with the promise of discovery and understanding. This chapter is your compass, guiding you through the step-by-step process of navigating the complex, yet rewarding, world of data.

Before diving into the depths, one must know why they are setting sail. The first step is to clearly define the objectives of your analysis. What questions are you seeking to answer? Is it to understand customer behavior, predict future trends, or improve operational efficiency? Setting clear, achievable goals is paramount, as it shapes the direction of your entire analysis.

Consider a library looking to increase membership. Their objective might be to understand the factors influencing signup rates. This clarity guides the subsequent steps, ensuring efforts are focused and relevant.

With objectives set, the next step is to assemble your crew - the data. Drawing from concepts in Chapter 5, data collection is both an art and a science. You must identify the sources of data that will help you answer your questions. These sources could be internal, like sales records, or external, such as social media analytics.

DATA DEMYSTIFIED: A BEGINNER'S GUIDE TO UNDERSTANDING THE WORLD THROUGH NUMBERS

Imagine a farmer wanting to boost crop yields. They might collect data on soil conditions, weather patterns, and crop varieties. Each piece of data acts like a crew member, playing a unique role in the journey ahead.

Not all crew members are ready for the journey. Some may be ill-equipped or carry inaccuracies that could hinder the voyage. Data cleaning is the process of preparing your crew, ensuring they are accurate and relevant. This involves removing duplicates, correcting errors, and dealing with missing values.

Think of a chef preparing ingredients for a dish. Just as bruised fruits are trimmed and washed, data too must be cleaned to ensure the analysis is based on the best possible information.

With a clean and prepared crew, it's time to chart the waters. Data exploration involves delving into your data to understand patterns, relationships, and anomalies. This step is crucial for gaining insights and guiding the analysis.

A detective piecing together clues from a crime scene is a fitting analogy. By examining the data from various angles, unexpected patterns might emerge, revealing new paths to explore.

The final step in our journey is data modeling, where we use statistical methods to predict outcomes or infer conclusions. This is where the magic happens - turning raw data into actionable insights.

Imagine an architect designing a building. Just as they create models to predict how a structure will stand, data modeling helps us predict future trends or understand underlying relationships. For instance, a retailer might use data modeling to predict which products will be best-sellers during the holiday season.

This step requires careful consideration of the methods used, as each model has its strengths and limitations. It's like choosing the right sail for the wind conditions; the choice can significantly impact the journey's success.

As the land comes into view, and the journey nears its end, it's essential to reflect on the voyage. Each step in the data analysis process is iterative. Insights gained might prompt a return to earlier steps for further exploration or refinement.

Data analysis is not a journey to a final destination but an ongoing voyage of discovery. With each dataset explored, new questions arise, leading to new journeys.

Data analysis is an adventure, one that requires curiosity, patience, and a willingness to explore the unknown. By following this step-by-step guide, you're not just analyzing data; you're uncovering the stories hidden within the numbers.

Remember, every piece of data is a star in the vast universe of information. And with the right tools and techniques, you can navigate these stars, uncovering insights and knowledge that can transform the world around you.

So, set your sights on the horizon, dear reader. A world of discovery awaits. Embrace the adventure of data analysis, and let the journey transform you.

Tools for Data Analysis

Embarking on the adventure of data analysis requires not just a keen mind but also the right set of tools. Like a skilled artisan, the choice of your instruments can significantly influence the quality and efficiency of your work. This chapter delves into the arsenal available for data analysts, guiding you through selecting the perfect tools for your journey.

Imagine standing at the edge of a dense forest, the canopy stretching endlessly before you. Your task is to map a path through this verdant expanse. In this scenario, Excel and Google Sheets are akin to a sturdy machete and a reliable compass. With these tools, basic yet versatile, you can begin charting a course through the data wilderness.

Excel, a stalwart in the realm of data analysis, offers a robust suite of features for sorting, filtering, and visualizing data. Its formulas and pivot tables allow for a comprehensive analysis, making sense of numbers in a way that stories begin to emerge from the spreadsheet. Excel's strength lies in its accessibility

DATA DEMYSTIFIED: A BEGINNER'S GUIDE TO UNDERSTANDING THE WORLD THROUGH NUMBERS

and familiarity; it's a tool many have wielded at some point, making initial forays into data analysis less daunting.

Google Sheets, on the other hand, thrives on collaboration. It invites multiple explorers to chart the same map simultaneously, each contributing from their corner of the world. Its real-time collaboration features ensure that insights and discoveries are shared instantly, fostering a spirit of teamwork and innovation.

As the journey progresses, the terrain becomes more challenging, requiring tools of greater sophistication. Enter R and Python, the precision tools in the data analyst's belt. Imagine you've moved from charting paths in the forest to navigating the stars. These languages, with their powerful libraries and packages, allow for complex statistical analysis and machine learning, offering insights not just on where you've been but also predicting where you could go.

R, with its origins in statistical analysis, shines brightly in data visualization and hypothesis testing. Its comprehensive array of packages, like ggplot2 for stunning data visuals and dplyr for data manipulation, makes it an invaluable ally in uncovering the stories hidden within the data.

Python, with its simplicity and versatility, has become the lingua franca of data analysis and machine learning. Libraries such as Pandas for data manipulation, NumPy for numerical computations, and Scikit-learn for machine learning transform Python into a Swiss knife for data scientists. Its syntax is intuitive, making the transition from data analyst to data scientist a journey of growth rather than a leap into the unknown.

How, then, does one choose the right tool? The answer lies in understanding the nature of your journey. For tasks requiring straightforward data cleaning and preliminary analysis, Excel and Google Sheets offer a solid starting point. Their simplicity and accessibility make them ideal for those at the beginning of their data analysis path.

But as the questions become more complex and the datasets larger, R and Python offer the computational power and flexibility required to navigate these advanced challenges. The choice between R and Python often comes down to personal preference and the specific requirements of the project at hand.

Beware, for the allure of sophisticated tools can lead one astray. A common pitfall is to leap into using R and Python without mastering the basics of data analysis. Excel and Google Sheets provide a foundation upon which one can build a strong understanding of data. They teach the principles of data exploration and visualization that are crucial, regardless of the tool used.

As you stand at the crossroads, tool in hand, remember that the journey of data analysis is one of perpetual learning. With each dataset unraveled and each insight uncovered, the horizon of your knowledge expands.

Let this chapter serve as a guide in selecting your tools, but let not the choice limit your journey. The world of data is vast and ever-changing. New tools and technologies emerge, each with the potential to transform the landscape of data analysis.

Embrace the adventure with an open mind and a curious heart. The path you chart through the world of data is unique, and the insights you uncover have the power to illuminate the unseen, to transform the abstract into the tangible.

So, take a deep breath, dear reader. The journey of data analysis awaits, a journey not just of numbers and charts, but of discovery and transformation. With the right tools in your belt and a spirit of exploration, there is no limit to the worlds you can unlock.

Practical Data Analysis Techniques

Embarking on the journey of understanding data is akin to learning a new language, a language spoken not through words but through numbers and patterns. This chapter, "Practical Data Analysis Techniques," aims to translate this numerical language into actionable insights, making the abstract tangible and the complex simple. It's a journey that begins with the basics: descriptive statistics, trend analysis, and comparative analysis. Through real-world datasets and simple exercises, we'll explore these techniques, turning numbers into narratives.

Imagine you're at a bustling market, a kaleidoscope of colors and activities swirling around you. Descriptive statistics are like taking a snapshot of this

DATA DEMYSTIFIED: A BEGINNER'S GUIDE TO UNDERSTANDING THE WORLD THROUGH NUMBERS

chaos, capturing the essence in a few key figures: the average price of goods, the most common items, and the range of products available. It simplifies the complex, providing a summary that tells a story of the market at a glance.

1. : These are the trio that describes the center of your data. The mean, or average, is like finding the balance point of a seesaw. The median, the middle value when your data is lined up, offers insight into the distribution's center, unaffected by outliers. The mode, the most frequent value, shows what's popular or common.

2. : These three musketeers of dispersion tell us about the spread of our data. The range gives the distance between the smallest and largest values. Variance digs deeper, measuring the average degree to which each point differs from the mean. Standard deviation, the square root of variance, provides a yardstick for comparing the spread of different datasets.

Let's put this into practice. Consider a dataset of monthly expenses for a year. By calculating the mean, we understand our average spending. The median reveals the midpoint of our expenses, and the mode may highlight our most common monthly expense. Variance and standard deviation, on the other hand, offer insights into the consistency of our spending patterns.

Trend analysis is akin to observing the seasons change from the same window over a year. It's about identifying patterns or trends in data over time. Are sales increasing as the months pass? Is the temperature rising year by year?

1. : These are the bread and butter of trend analysis. They plot data points on a graph and connect them with lines, making it easier to spot upward or downward trends.

2. : This technique smooths out short-term fluctuations, making it easier to see long-term trends. It's like looking at the forest, not just the individual trees.

Consider a dataset of daily temperatures for a year. By plotting these on a line graph, we can visually inspect for trends, such as increasing temperatures during summer. Applying a moving average, perhaps over a 7-day period, smooths out anomalies like an unseasonably warm day in winter, allowing us to see the broader warming trend as spring approaches.

Comparative analysis is the detective work of data analysis, looking for clues that reveal differences or similarities between datasets. It's the method used when we ask questions like, "Do students perform better on tests after attending review sessions?"

1. : These tools compare quantities across different categories or distributions within a single category. They are the magnifying glass that helps us see these differences more clearly.

2. : These statistical tests take comparative analysis further, determining if the differences we see are statistically significant or if they could have happened by chance.

Imagine we have test scores from two groups of students: those who attended review sessions and those who did not. By using bar charts, we can visually compare the average scores of both groups. Conducting a T-test would allow us to determine if the observed difference in scores is significant or not.

Data analysis is not a destination but a journey. It's a process of exploration, of asking questions, and seeking answers in the sea of numbers. Through descriptive statistics, we summarize and understand the essence of our data. Trend analysis allows us to observe changes over time, revealing the stories behind the numbers. Comparative analysis uncovers differences and similarities, providing insights into the effects of various factors.

Now, dear reader, armed with these techniques, you are ready to embark on your own journey of discovery through data. Remember, the beauty of data analysis lies not just in the numbers but in the stories they tell and the decisions they inform. So, dive in, explore, and let the data speak.

Interpreting and Presenting Analysis Results

Interpreting and presenting analysis results stands as the beacon that illuminates the path from raw data to actionable insights. This phase transforms

DATA DEMYSTIFIED: A BEGINNER'S GUIDE TO UNDERSTANDING THE WORLD THROUGH NUMBERS

the numerical language we've deciphered into narratives that resonate with our audience, regardless of their expertise in data analysis. It's a delicate art, balancing clarity with complexity, simplicity with depth. Here, we delve into the essentials of interpreting results and crafting presentations that not only inform but also inspire.

Interpretation begins where calculation ends. It's a critical step, akin to reading between the lines of a poem, seeking the underlying meaning rather than just appreciating its rhythm. But how do we extract the story our data is trying to tell?

Start by revisiting your objectives. Each analysis was performed with a question in mind. Does the result answer this question? If the data reveals an unexpected trend, explore it. Curiosity drives deeper understanding. Remember, anomalies might be the windows to new insights.

Consider the context. Numbers don't exist in a vacuum. A sudden spike in social media engagement might coincide with a marketing campaign or a viral event. Without context, interpretations can mislead.

Reflect on the implications. What do these findings mean for your organization or field of study? How do they influence decisions? Interpreting data is not just about understanding what is, but envisioning what could be.

Once you've gleaned insights from your data, the next challenge is presenting them. Your goal? To communicate findings in a way that's accessible, engaging, and persuasive.

Select the right visualization tools. A well-chosen graph can speak volumes. Line graphs illustrate trends over time, while pie charts break down parts of a whole. Choose the tool that best conveys your message. But remember, simplicity reigns supreme. Overly complex charts can confuse rather than clarify.

Tailor your presentation to your audience. A room full of statisticians will have different expectations than a group of marketing executives. Use technical language judiciously. When in doubt, simplify. Your aim is to enlighten, not alienate.

Storytelling with data is your most powerful tool. Humans are hardwired for stories. They engage us emotionally, making the abstract tangible. Begin with a compelling question, present your data as the protagonist, and guide your audience through the narrative arc to the conclusion. This journey, properly structured, makes your insights memorable and actionable.

Clear, concise communication is the bedrock of effective presentation. Avoid jargon and opt for simplicity. Use vivid imagery to bring your data to life. Instead of saying, "Sales increased by 20%," paint a picture: "Imagine every seat in our city's largest theater filled – that's how many more people chose our product this year."

Engage your audience with direct questions. "What would a 10% increase in customer satisfaction mean for our business?" These queries invite listeners to participate in the narrative, making the data relevant to their experiences.

Employ a varied sentence structure. Mix short, impactful statements with longer, descriptive ones to create a rhythm that keeps your audience engaged.

Consider this one-line paragraph for emphasis: Data tells a story. Yours.

Limit the use of adverbs and adjectives. Instead, let strong verbs and nouns do the heavy lifting. "The sales figures soared," is more powerful than, "The sales figures were very good."

Interpreting and presenting data analysis results are not merely the final steps in our journey but the bridge connecting insights to action. By mastering these skills, you transform from a data analyst into a data storyteller, wielding the power to influence decisions and inspire change.

Remember, the goal is not just to present numbers but to weave them into a narrative that resonates, persuades, and enlightens. Whether you're addressing experts or novices, your ability to demystify data determines the impact of your insights.

In the realm of data analysis, the story is the thing. Let yours be one that not only informs but also inspires and ignites action.

Common Pitfalls and How to Avoid Them

In the realm of data analysis, the path to enlightenment is fraught with potential missteps. Understanding the common pitfalls and learning how to sidestep them is crucial for anyone aspiring to master the art of data interpretation. Let us delve into these treacherous territories, illuminating the way for safer passage through the numbers that encapsulate our world.

In the quest for accuracy, it's tempting to construct models that cling too tightly to the data. This phenomenon, known as overfitting, results in models that perform exceptionally well on the data they were trained on but falter miserably when introduced to new information. Picture a tailor crafting a suit so precisely to one individual that it becomes unwearable for anyone else.

How, then, can we avoid this trap? Simplicity is our guiding principle. When building models, strive for the simplest explanation that adequately captures the phenomenon of interest. Employ techniques like cross-validation, where the data is divided into parts, with some used for training and some for testing, ensuring the model's performance is robust across different datasets.

Outliers, data points that deviate markedly from the rest, are often dismissed as anomalies or errors. However, ignoring these outliers can be akin to overlooking buried treasure. Sometimes, these data points reveal new insights or flaws in our data collection methods.

To navigate this pitfall, adopt a mindset of curiosity. Instead of immediately discarding outliers, investigate them. Determine whether they're the result of errors or if they hold valuable information. This approach ensures that we don't miss out on potentially groundbreaking insights hidden within the data's fringes.

The excitement of uncovering patterns can sometimes lead us to draw conclusions prematurely, basing our findings on an inadequate data sample. This is akin to tasting a single grain of rice and declaring the entire pot ready.

The safeguard against this error is patience. Accumulate enough data to ensure that the patterns observed are not mere flukes. Statistical tests can help determine whether the findings are likely to hold up across larger datasets. Always question the validity of your conclusions, especially when working with limited data.

Adopting a critical, questioning mindset is your best defense against the myriad pitfalls in data analysis. With each step, ask yourself whether the assumptions you're making are justified and whether alternative explanations could account for your findings. This reflective practice helps safeguard against errors and biases that can lead us astray.

No analysis is complete without the scrutiny of peer review. Sharing your findings with colleagues or within your professional community invites constructive criticism that can fortify your conclusions. Collaboration brings diverse perspectives, shedding light on potential oversights and introducing new angles of interpretation.

Remember, the journey of data analysis is one of perpetual learning. Each dataset tells a new story, offering lessons and challenges. By recognizing and learning from the common pitfalls, you equip yourself with the wisdom to navigate the complexities of data with greater assurance.

In conclusion, the path to demystifying data is fraught with potential missteps, but with the right approach, these pitfalls can become opportunities for growth. Embrace a critical, questioning mindset, value the insights gained from collaboration, and always strive for clarity and simplicity in your models. This way, you'll not only avoid common errors but also unlock the true power of data to illuminate the world around us.

Data tells a story. Let yours be one of accuracy, insight, and enlightenment.

Making Decisions With Data

The Role of Data in Informed Decision-Making

In today's world, where intuition often guides the helm of decision-making, a seismic shift is underway. This transformation, powered by the meticulous collection and analysis of data, is changing the landscape of how decisions are made, from the floors of retail giants to the desks of public health officials.

Imagine a bustling retail store, its shelves lined with an array of products, from the latest fashion trends to the most sought-after electronics. In the not-so-distant past, the manager might have relied on gut feelings or past experiences to predict which items would fly off the shelves. Now, picture a world where every purchase, every return, and even every online click is meticulously recorded and analyzed. This data becomes a beacon, guiding the manager in optimizing inventory levels, not based on intuition, but on hard, actionable data. The result? Shelves that rarely empty and a reduction in overstocked items gathering dust.

But the power of data extends far beyond the retail sector.

Consider the realm of public health, where decisions can mean the difference between life and death. In the face of a burgeoning health crisis, public health officials no longer need to rely solely on historical outbreaks or generalized models. Instead, they turn to real-time epidemiological data, tracking the spread of diseases with precision, identifying hotspots, and allocating resources with a previously unattainable accuracy. Here, data doesn't just inform decisions; it saves lives.

But how precisely does data-driven decision-making eclipse the intuition-based approaches of yore?

At its core, data reduces uncertainty. Every decision, from the mundane to the monumental, involves some level of guesswork. By leveraging data, this guesswork is minimized, replaced by insights drawn from patterns, trends, and correlations. For instance, a farmer using data analytics to monitor soil moisture levels can make informed decisions about irrigation, significantly improving crop yield. This isn't guesswork; it's precision farming.

Data also plays a pivotal role in reducing bias. Human decision-making is fraught with biases, often subconscious, that can skew perceptions and lead to less-than-optimal outcomes. Data, when collected and analyzed objectively, offers a bulwark against these biases, providing a more neutral foundation upon which to base decisions. A hiring manager, for example, might unconsciously favor candidates from a particular alma mater. A data-driven recruitment process, on the other hand, focuses on metrics that matter, such as skills test scores and past performance indicators, ensuring a fairer and more equitable selection process.

But what about the skeptics?

Some argue that data-driven decision-making depersonalizes the process, stripping away the human element that brings warmth and intuition to the table. To them, we pose a question: Is it not possible that data, in its objectivity, allows us to make decisions that are not only smarter but also more compassionate? When a hospital administrator uses patient flow data to improve the efficiency of care, is that not a deeply human decision, one that reduces wait times and potentially saves lives?

Perhaps one of the most compelling examples of data's transformative power is seen in the realm of environmental conservation. Scientists and conservationists use data to monitor changes in climate patterns, track endangered species, and assess the health of ecosystems. This data informs everything from policy decisions to conservation strategies, enabling a targeted approach to protecting our planet.

In conclusion, the role of data in informed decision-making cannot be overstated. It is a tool of unparalleled power, one that has the potential to transform intuition-based approaches into methodologies grounded in evidence and objectivity. Through vivid examples from retail, public health, agriculture, recruitment, and environmental conservation, we see that data not only informs decisions but, in many cases, makes them better.

Let us embrace this shift, recognizing the value of data in reducing uncertainty, combating bias, and enhancing our decision-making processes. After all, in a world awash with data, the ability to harness its power is not just an advantage; it's a necessity.

In the chapters that follow, we will delve deeper into the methodologies of data collection and analysis, exploring the tools and techniques that make this transformation possible. Join us on this journey through the world of numbers, and let us demystify data together.

Frameworks for Data-Informed Decisions

Embarking on the path of data-informed decision-making is akin to setting sail on uncharted waters. The vast sea of data, with its potential to guide us to informed choices, can seem overwhelming. Yet, with the right frameworks and methodologies, navigating these waters becomes less daunting, more directed. This chapter delves into structured approaches such as the OODA Loop and SWOT Analysis, tailored for a data-driven context, alongside other strategic planning tools. These frameworks are not merely theoretical constructs; they are practical guides that, when applied, illuminate the path to insightful, data-informed decisions.

Imagine standing at a crossroads, with multiple paths unfurling before you. The OODA Loop, a concept originally developed by military strategist John Boyd, offers a compass. In its essence, the OODA Loop encompasses four stages: Observe, Orient, Decide, Act. This cyclical process starts with observing the available data, which could range from market trends to customer feedback. But how does one move from observation to orientation?

Here lies the crux. To orient is to understand the implications of the data within the context of your objectives and constraints. It involves analyzing the data, identifying patterns, and discerning opportunities or threats. This step transforms raw data into actionable insights. But what comes next? Decision making. Armed with insights, you're prepared to choose a course of action. Finally, the act stage involves implementing the decision and monitoring its outcomes, which feeds back into observation, and the loop begins anew.

Now, let's paint a scenario. A startup aims to launch a new product. By applying the OODA Loop, the team systematically analyzes market data, competitor performance, and customer preferences. This structured approach not only guides them to a well-informed decision but also enables rapid adaptation to new information or outcomes, a critical advantage in the fast-paced business world.

Moving beyond the OODA Loop, another invaluable framework for data-informed decision-making is the SWOT Analysis. Tailored for a data-driven context, it involves identifying Strengths, Weaknesses, Opportunities, and Threats related to a particular decision or project. But how does one tailor this framework to leverage data effectively?

The answer lies in the systematic collection and analysis of data for each component of SWOT. Strengths and weaknesses are internal factors; hence, the focus is on internal data such as performance metrics or employee skills. Opportunities and threats, being external, require analyzing external data, such as market trends or regulatory changes. A vivid example could be a retail company assessing its e-commerce platform. Through SWOT, data reveals strengths in user experience but weaknesses in payment security. Simultaneously, it highlights opportunities in expanding to emerging markets and threats from increasing cyber-attacks. This holistic view, grounded in data, enables the company to make strategic decisions that capitalize on strengths, mitigate weaknesses, address threats, and pursue opportunities.

But is there a one-size-fits-all approach?

Certainly not. The complexity of decision-making scenarios varies, necessitating the application of these frameworks with flexibility and creativity. Consider a small business facing a straightforward decision, like selecting a new supplier. Here, a simplified OODA Loop might suffice. In contrast, a multinational corporation strategizing for global expansion might combine an in-depth SWOT Analysis with the OODA Loop for comprehensive planning.

Through vivid imagery, let's envision a world where every decision, be it small or monumental, is informed by data. A world where businesses, governments, and individuals harness the power of structured frameworks to navigate the vast sea of data. This vision is not only achievable but necessary in our data-driven era.

In conclusion, the journey through data-informed decision-making is transformative. By adopting frameworks like the OODA Loop and SWOT Analysis, tailored for a data-driven context, decision-makers are equipped to navigate the complexities of the modern world. These methodologies serve as beacons, guiding us through the fog of uncertainty, towards informed, strategic decisions. As we delve deeper into the realms of data analytics in the subsequent chapters, let us hold fast to these frameworks, our reliable compasses in the ever-evolving landscape of data.

Remember, the power of data-informed decision-making lies not in the data itself, but in how we interpret, analyze, and act upon it. Let this chapter serve as a foundation, empowering you to harness the full potential of data in your decision-making processes.

Balancing Data With Intuition

In the preceding chapter, we ventured through the structured landscapes of OODA Loop and SWOT Analysis, illuminating a path for data-informed decision-making. But a question lingers, echoing in the chambers of our minds: Is data the sole compass guiding us through the decision-making process? The answer unfolds in this chapter, as we explore the delicate balance between data insights and human intuition, emphasizing that data should inform, not replace, human judgment.

Imagine a seasoned gardener, her hands caressing the soil, her eyes discerning the subtle signs of a plant's needs. She draws upon years of experience, an intuitive understanding of her garden that no dataset can fully capture. Yet, she also embraces technology, using moisture sensors and climate data to inform her decisions. This harmony between intuition and data mirrors the balance we seek in decision-making across fields far and wide.

Why, then, is balancing data with intuition crucial? Data, with its quantitative might, offers a lens to view patterns, trends, and correlations. It equips us with evidence, reducing uncertainty in our decisions. However, data is not infallible. It can be incomplete, biased, or misleading. Moreover, data lacks the ability to comprehend the nuances of human emotions, ethics, and the intricacies of cultural contexts. Here, intuition steps in, bridging the gap. Intuition, shaped by experience, empathy, and tacit knowledge, allows us to read between the lines, to sense what data cannot quantify.

Consider the tale of a renowned chef crafting a new dish. While data informs him of popular flavors and dietary trends, it is his intuition that guides the delicate balance of ingredients, creating a symphony of tastes. Similarly, in business, while data analytics might suggest a promising market for expansion, it is the leader's intuition, honed by years of experience, that senses the timing and strategy for such a move.

How then, do we achieve this balance? The integration of qualitative insights with quantitative data analysis is key. This approach requires fostering an environment where data scientists and domain experts collaborate, valuing each other's insights. Let's delve into a case study that exemplifies this successful integration.

In the healthcare sector, a hospital aimed to reduce patient readmission rates. Data analysis identified patterns and high-risk factors associated with readmissions. However, it was the nurses' and doctors' intuitive understanding of patient behavior and their informal conversations with patients that uncovered a critical insight: many readmissions were due to patients not taking their medications correctly. This blend of quantitative data and qualitative insights led to the implementation of personalized patient education programs, significantly reducing readmission rates.

This story illustrates a pivotal lesson: data provides the what, while intuition often uncovers the why. To foster this balance, organizations must cultivate a culture of curiosity, encouraging questions that challenge the data and the status quo. Training in critical thinking and judgment becomes as vital as training in data analytics.

But how do we ensure that intuition does not become a guise for bias or resistance to change? Here, a structured approach to integrating intuition with data is beneficial. It involves:

1. : Use data to test and validate intuitive hunches.

2. : Keep a record of decisions made based on intuition and their outcomes. This builds a repository of experiential learning.

3. : Encourage cross-functional teams to discuss and debate data insights and intuitive perspectives.

4. : Regularly reflect on decisions made, examining the role of data and intuition in their success or failure.

In the dance of decision-making, data and intuition are partners, each leading at times, but always in sync. As we embrace this partnership, we unlock the full spectrum of insights, from the tangible to the tacit.

Remember the gardener and the chef, their stories a testament to the power of balancing data with intuition. Like them, let us navigate the world of decision-making with both the compass of data and the intuition that whispers in the winds of experience.

In our journey through the world of data, this chapter stands as a beacon, reminding us that the heart and the mind must journey together, informing and enriching each other. As we continue, let us carry forward the lesson that in the symphony of decision-making, data and intuition harmonize to create a melody that guides us to informed, holistic, and wise decisions.

Thus, as we delve further into understanding the world through numbers, let's not forget the human element, the intuition that colors data with the shades of our experiences and values. Balancing data with intuition is not just an art; it's a science, one that we can all learn and improve upon, making our decisions not just smart, but wise.

Overcoming Challenges in Data-Driven Decision-

Making

Embarking on the path of data-driven decision-making is akin to navigating a vast and often tumultuous sea. While the previous chapter illuminated the synergy between data and intuition, it's crucial to address the storms that may arise: common challenges encountered in the realm of data-driven decision-making. These challenges, ranging from data quality issues to analysis paralysis and organizational resistance to change, often act as formidable barriers. However, like any seasoned navigator, we must learn to overcome these obstacles, charting a course towards a more informed and data-savvy future.

Imagine setting sail across the ocean, relying on a map littered with inaccuracies. Just as such a map can lead a ship astray, poor quality data can derail decision-making processes. Data quality issues, including inaccuracies, incompleteness, and inconsistencies, represent a hidden iceberg on our journey.

How, then, can we navigate these treacherous waters? Establishing robust data governance is akin to having a skilled lookout on the mast. This involves setting clear policies and standards for data collection, storage, and usage, ensuring that data is accurate, complete, and consistent. But it's not just about setting rules; it's about cultivating a culture that values data quality. This means every member of the organization must understand their role in maintaining the integrity of data, from the moment it's collected to its final use in decision-making.

Another challenge is the seductive lure of analysis paralysis, where the quest for perfect insights becomes a siren's call, leading us away from timely decision-making. In the quest for precision, it's easy to become ensnared in an endless cycle of analysis, constantly seeking more data and never reaching a decision.

To overcome this, setting realistic expectations for data projects is critical. It involves understanding that perfection is often the enemy of progress. Decisions need not always be made with complete certainty; they can be iterative, evolving with new data and insights. Encouraging a mindset of 'good enough' can free us from the chains of analysis paralysis, allowing us to navigate with agility and confidence.

Resistance to change within organizations is the Leviathan we must battle. Often, this resistance stems from a fear of the unknown, a comfortable adherence to status quo, or a lack of data literacy. Overcoming this requires fostering a culture of data literacy, where data is not seen as a threat but as a valuable tool for improvement.

This involves not only providing training on how to interpret and use data but also demonstrating the tangible benefits of data-driven decision-making. Success stories, where data initiatives have led to positive outcomes, can serve as powerful beacons, illuminating the path forward. Furthermore, involving all levels of the organization in data initiatives, making data accessible, and transparent can demystify data, turning resistance into acceptance.

The data landscape is ever-evolving, with new technologies, methodologies, and types of data emerging. Embracing continuous learning and adaptation is therefore not just beneficial; it's essential.

This requires a commitment to staying abreast of developments in the field of data analytics and an openness to experimenting with new approaches. Encouraging a culture of innovation, where trial and error are seen as pathways to discovery, can foster an environment ripe for continuous improvement.

In conclusion, while the journey towards data-driven decision-making is fraught with challenges, it is also filled with opportunities for growth and improvement. By establishing clear data governance, fostering a culture of data literacy, setting realistic expectations, and embracing continuous learning, we can navigate these challenges successfully.

Let us then set our sights on the horizon, ready to face the storms with resilience and to chart a course towards a future where data not only informs our decisions but empowers them. As we continue to demystify the world of data, let us remember that the journey itself is a part of the destination, a continuous loop of learning, adapting, and evolving.

Ethical Considerations in Data-Driven Decisions

With the compass of our journey set towards understanding the ethical landscape of data-driven decisions, we embark on a critical exploration. This voyage takes us beyond the mechanics of data analysis, charting a course into the heart of ethical considerations that are paramount in leveraging data responsibly. As we delve into this territory, it becomes evident that the power of data comes with profound responsibilities.

In an era where data is as abundant as the ocean's waters, the line between insightful analysis and privacy invasion becomes increasingly blurred. Consider the scenario where companies collect personal data under the guise of improving customer experience. Here, the question arises: At what point does the pursuit of data-driven insights infringe upon individual privacy?

To navigate these murky waters, guidelines on data minimization and consent are akin to lighthouses guiding ships to safe harbor. Data minimization, the practice of collecting only what is necessary, ensures that the invasion of privacy is not an unintended consequence of data collection. Similarly, obtaining explicit consent from individuals before collecting their data acts as a safeguard, ensuring that the individuals' rights are respected.

Bias in data is a treacherous current that can lead decisions astray. It stems from a multitude of sources - historical data reflecting past inequalities, biased algorithms, or even the manner in which data is collected. The result? Decisions that perpetuate inequality or injustice.

The fight against biased data requires a vigilant and multifaceted approach. Auditing data for bias, employing diverse teams that can spot and challenge prejudiced assumptions, and continuously monitoring outcomes for unintended disparities are crucial steps. By acknowledging and addressing bias, we strive to ensure that our data-driven decisions do not reinforce the very issues we seek to solve.

Every decision made on the basis of data sends ripples through communities, affecting various stakeholders in ways that may not be immediately apparent.

Ignoring the broader societal implications of these decisions is akin to navigating a ship without considering the marine life below.

For instance, consider the deployment of automated decision-making systems in areas like hiring or law enforcement. Without careful consideration, these systems can adversely affect certain groups, reinforcing existing disparities. Engaging with stakeholders, understanding their concerns, and incorporating their perspectives into decision-making processes ensure that the decisions made are not just data-driven but also socially responsible.

To steer the ship of data-driven decision-making responsibly, certain guidelines must be followed. Transparency about how data is collected, used, and shared builds trust and accountability. Decisions should be explainable, with individuals able to understand how and why a decision affecting them was made. Moreover, an ethical approach to data use involves constant vigilance, with organizations ready to reassess and adjust their practices in light of new information or changing societal norms.

One cannot overstate the importance of fostering an ethical culture within organizations. This culture champions not just compliance with regulations but a deeper commitment to doing what is right in the realm of data usage. Training programs, ethical audits, and open discussions about ethical dilemmas should be part of the fabric of any organization aspiring to make data-driven decisions responsibly.

Let this chapter serve as a beacon, illuminating the path towards ethical data use. The journey does not end here; it requires ongoing commitment and vigilance. As we continue to harness the power of data, let us do so with a keen awareness of the ethical dimensions involved.

Imagine a world where data-driven decisions are made with consideration for privacy, free from bias, mindful of their impact on all stakeholders, and guided by a clear ethical compass. This is the world we aspire to create.

In our hands lies the power to shape this future. The question now is, will we rise to the challenge?

The journey of understanding and leveraging data is complex, filled with opportunities and pitfalls. As we navigate this landscape, let us remember that at the heart of every dataset, every analysis, and every decision, lie the values we choose to uphold.

Case Studies: Data-Driven Success Stories

In the vast expanse of the digital age, where data acts as the North Star guiding businesses towards uncharted territories of opportunity, several pioneers have harnessed its luminous glow to navigate their way to success. Their journeys, marked by challenges, innovation, and strategic acumen, stand as beacons for others to follow. Let us delve into these stories, drawing inspiration and practical insights from their experiences.

Imagine walking into a fashion store where the shelves refresh with new designs faster than the seasons change. This is the reality at Zara, a titan in the fast-fashion industry, whose success story is woven with threads of data.

Zara's designers don't just rely on intuition; they listen to the silent whispers of data. Sales figures, customer feedback, and even real-time observations from store employees feed into a sophisticated algorithm. This data-driven approach allows Zara to predict trends before they happen and adjust their inventory accordingly, ensuring that what you see on the rack is always in vogue.

But Zara's mastery of data doesn't stop at forecasting trends. The company has perfected the art of the quick turnaround, transforming raw data into wearable fashion in record time. This agility is a testament to the power of integrating data across every link of the supply chain, from design to delivery.

The lesson? In the fast-paced world of retail, success belongs to those who can anticipate change and act swiftly, guided by the compass of data.

How did a startup redefine urban mobility and grow to dominate the streets of cities around the globe? Uber's journey from a simple idea to a transportation behemoth is a masterclass in leveraging data.

DATA DEMYSTIFIED: A BEGINNER'S GUIDE TO UNDERSTANDING THE WORLD THROUGH NUMBERS

Uber's app, a gateway to millions of rides daily, collects vast amounts of data, painting a detailed picture of urban mobility. This data is the fuel that powers Uber's engine, optimizing routes, predicting demand, and setting dynamic pricing. The result? A service that's not just convenient but almost psychic in its ability to meet users' needs.

But Uber's data-driven strategy extends beyond the app. The company uses data to address challenges such as traffic congestion and pollution, partnering with cities to create smarter, more sustainable urban environments.

The takeaway? Data can drive not just business success but also positive change, transforming how we live and move.

In the conservative world of banking, Capital One stands out as a maverick, rewriting the rules of finance with a secret weapon: data analytics.

Capital One's journey began with a bold question: Could data predict an individual's creditworthiness better than traditional methods? The answer, it turned out, was a resounding yes. By mining data for insights into consumer behavior, Capital One was able to offer credit cards tailored to individual risk profiles, revolutionizing the industry.

But the company didn't stop there. Capital One embraced data analytics across its operations, from fraud detection to customer service, always seeking ways to use data to enhance the customer experience and streamline operations.

The moral of the story? In an industry built on numbers, those who can decipher the stories data tells hold the key to innovation and competitive advantage.

At the Mayo Clinic, data is more than numbers on a screen; it's a lifeline that guides decisions in the high-stakes world of healthcare.

The clinic's commitment to data-driven decision-making is perhaps best exemplified by its pioneering work in predictive analytics. By analyzing vast datasets, the Mayo Clinic can predict which patients are at risk of developing certain conditions, allowing for early intervention and better outcomes.

Moreover, the Mayo Clinic leverages data to personalize treatment, tailoring interventions to the unique genetic makeup of each patient. This approach, known as precision medicine, represents the future of healthcare, promising treatments that are as unique as the patients themselves.

What can we learn from the Mayo Clinic's story? That in the quest to save lives, data is an invaluable ally, offering insights that can shape more effective, personalized care.

In these stories, we see a common thread: the transformative power of data. From fashion to transportation, banking to healthcare, data-driven decision-making has paved the way for innovation, efficiency, and success. As we stand on the brink of a future where data's potential is limitless, let us take inspiration from these pioneers, embracing the challenges and opportunities that lie ahead.

Are you ready to write your own data-driven success story?

Data in Business

Harnessing Data for Strategic Advantage

In the digital age, data reigns supreme. From the bustling streets of Silicon Valley to the traditional boardrooms of old-school conglomerates, the quest for data-driven insights has become the Holy Grail of modern business practices. This relentless pursuit stems from a simple truth: in data lies the power to not only predict the future but to create it.

Imagine, if you will, a small startup nestled in a cozy corner of a bustling city. Its ambitions are as vast as the data it seeks to harness. Through meticulous analysis, this fledgling company identifies an untapped market niche. Suddenly, what was once a mere idea begins to take shape, fuelled by the lifeblood of strategic data. This is the transformative magic of data at work, a phenomenon that is reshaping business models across the globe.

But how, you might ask, do businesses leverage this intangible asset to carve out a competitive edge? The answer lies in the myriad ways data can be dissected, interpreted, and applied. By sifting through mountains of information, companies can discern patterns, predict consumer behavior, and optimize their operations. A restaurant chain, for example, might analyze social media trends to determine the next big flavor sensation, thereby staying one step ahead of the culinary curve.

Equally crucial is the role of data in personalizing customer experiences. In a world awash with options, personalization is the key to capturing hearts and wallets. Consider the online retailer that recommends products based on your past purchases and browsing habits. This isn't just convenience; it's a tailored shopping experience, meticulously crafted from your digital footprint.

Yet, the power of data extends beyond market trends and personalized shopping carts. It is also a catalyst for operational efficiency. Airlines, for instance, harness data to optimize flight paths, reducing fuel consumption and minimizing delays. Here, data not only bolsters the bottom line but also contributes to a greener planet.

But let's pause for a moment.

Why is this important?

In a landscape where competition is fierce and innovation rapid, the strategic use of data can be the difference between thriving and merely surviving. It's about making informed decisions, reducing risks, and seizing opportunities. It's about not just knowing your customer but anticipating their needs.

The implications are profound. Businesses that fail to embrace the data revolution risk falling by the wayside, overtaken by nimbler, more data-savvy competitors. The message is clear: in the modern marketplace, data is not just an asset; it is an imperative.

Yet, for all its promise, the path to data mastery is fraught with challenges. The sheer volume of information can be overwhelming. Data privacy concerns loom large, and the ethical implications of data usage are a minefield of complexity. Moreover, translating data into actionable insights requires a blend of skills that are in short supply.

So, where does this leave us?

In the final analysis, the strategic advantage conferred by data is not just about possessing it. It's about the wisdom to use it judaniciously, the creativity to see beyond the numbers, and the ethical compass to use it responsibly. It is about building a culture that values data-driven decision-making while recognizing the human element behind the data points.

The journey to data enlightenment is neither quick nor easy. But for those willing to embark on it, the rewards are as vast as the data universe itself. In this brave new world, the dataphiles are the new pioneers, charting courses through uncharted territories, driven by the belief that in data lies the key to unlocking the mysteries of the market and the human psyche.

Thus, as we stand on the precipice of this data-driven era, one thing is abundantly clear: the future belongs to those who understand that data is not just a tool but a beacon that guides us toward innovation, efficiency, and, ultimately, a deeper connection with the world around us.

Harnessing data for strategic advantage is not just a business imperative; it is the cornerstone of a new paradigm where numbers illuminate the path to progress, prosperity, and a better understanding of our place in the digital cosmos.

Understanding Market Trends and Customer Behavior

In this evolving landscape, the art of understanding market trends and customer behavior through the lens of data analytics unfolds as a narrative rich with insights and opportunities. The journey into the heart of analytics reveals the methodologies that businesses employ to not just navigate but also shape the marketplace. Let's delve deeper into this fascinating world, where numbers narrate stories, predict futures, and unveil the desires of consumers.

Why, one might wonder, do businesses invest such significant resources in deciphering market trends and customer behavior? The answer is as straightforward as it is compelling: knowledge is power. In the context of business, this power translates into the ability to make informed decisions, tailor marketing strategies, and ultimately, drive profitability. At the core of this power lies the ability to segment customers effectively.

Customer segmentation, a critical aspect of data analytics, involves dividing a business's customer base into groups of individuals that are similar in specific ways relevant to marketing, such as age, gender, interests, and spending habits. But it's not just about grouping similar individuals together. It's about understanding what makes each segment tick. Here, data analytics steps in, transforming raw data into a rich tapestry of insights.

Imagine a local bookstore that, through analyzing purchase histories and customer feedback, identifies a significant segment of customers with a keen interest in science fiction. Armed with this insight, the bookstore tailors its inventory, hosts themed events, and even launches a science fiction book club. The result? A deeper connection with customers, increased loyalty, and, yes, enhanced profitability.

At the heart of predicting consumer preferences lies the concept of customer lifetime value (CLV). CLV represents the total worth to a business of a customer over the whole period of their relationship. It's an important metric because acquiring new customers is generally more costly than retaining existing ones. By focusing on maximizing the CLV of their customer base, businesses can optimize their marketing efforts and ensure long-term sustainability.

But how do businesses predict which customers will have the highest CLV? Enter predictive analytics, a discipline that uses data, statistical algorithms, and machine learning techniques to identify the likelihood of future outcomes based on historical data. A clothing retailer, for example, might use predictive analytics to determine which customers are most likely to respond to a new line of products, thereby crafting targeted marketing campaigns that resonate with those individuals.

Equally vital to understanding customer behavior is the net promoter score (NPS), a metric that measures customer loyalty and satisfaction. By asking a simple question – "How likely are you to recommend our company/product/service to a friend or colleague?" – businesses can gauge the loyalty of their customer base. A high NPS indicates satisfied customers who are likely to act as brand ambassadors, while a low NPS signals the need for improvement.

But what drives customer satisfaction? Often, it's the personalized experiences that businesses offer. In an era where consumers are bombarded with choices, personalization has emerged as a key differentiator. Data analytics enables businesses to craft personalized experiences by predicting what customers want before they even know it themselves. The online retailer that suggests products based on past purchases is not just selling more; it's creating a bespoke shopping experience for each customer.

Pause for a moment and consider the implications of such personalized experiences. They represent a shift from a one-size-fits-all approach to a nuanced understanding of individual preferences and behaviors. This shift is not merely about selling more products; it's about forging deeper, more meaningful connections with customers.

In crafting targeted marketing strategies, businesses leverage sophisticated analytics to slice through the noise of the marketplace and speak directly to the desires of their consumers. These strategies are not based on guesswork but on solid data-driven insights that illuminate the path forward.

But let's not forget: data analytics is not a panacea. It requires a commitment to ethical practices, a dedication to protecting customer privacy, and a recognition of the limitations of data. It demands a blend of technical skills and human judgment, a marriage of numbers and narratives.

In conclusion, the journey through the realm of data analytics reveals a landscape where understanding market trends and customer behavior is both an art and a science. It's a world where data not only informs business decisions but also enriches the customer experience, creating a virtuous cycle of engagement, loyalty, and growth. As we navigate this world, one truth remains clear: in the intricate dance of numbers and narratives, those who master the art of data analytics hold the key to unlocking unparalleled opportunities and insights.

Operational Efficiency and Innovation

In the quest for operational efficiency and innovation, businesses are increasingly turning to data analytics. This transformative approach not only streamlines operations but also paves the way for groundbreaking innovations. Through the lens of data, companies are redefining what it means to be efficient and innovative in a competitive market landscape.

Imagine a manufacturing plant where machines predict their own maintenance schedules, or a supply chain so optimized that products seem to move with almost precognitive foresight. These scenarios are not remnants of a futuristic novel but tangible realities in today's data-driven world.

How do companies achieve such feats? The journey begins with the meticulous collection and analysis of data. Consider the case of a global retailer that revolutionized its supply chain operations. By integrating data analytics into its logistics network, the retailer was able to predict market demands with unprecedented accuracy. This foresight allowed for real-time adjustments in inventory and delivery schedules, minimizing waste and maximizing efficiency. The result was a seamless flow of products from warehouse to customer, a testament to the power of data in transforming operations.

But operational efficiency is only one side of the coin. The other side sparkles with the brilliance of innovation. Data analytics not only streamlines existing processes but also uncovers opportunities for new products and services. A compelling example is a tech company that harnessed customer usage data to identify unmet needs. Through sophisticated data analysis, it unveiled patterns that pointed to a demand for a new type of product. The company swiftly pivoted its product development strategy, resulting in a groundbreaking offering that captured the market's imagination.

Such stories underscore a vital lesson: data is more than numbers; it's a source of insight and inspiration.

But where do the challenges lie? Accurately predicting maintenance schedules, for instance, requires a deep dive into vast oceans of data, from machine performance logs to environmental conditions. Predictive maintenance, as this practice is known, leverages advanced algorithms to forecast equipment failures before they occur. The benefits are multifold: reduced downtime, lower maintenance costs, and prolonged equipment life. A leading aerospace manufacturer reported saving millions annually by implementing predictive maintenance strategies, showcasing the profound impact of data analytics on operational costs.

In the realm of product development, the narrative is equally compelling. Data analytics enables companies to understand consumer behavior with granular precision. This understanding leads to products that resonate deeply with target audiences, ensuring not just market success but also customer loyalty. A notable success story involves a beverage company that used social media data to identify emerging flavor trends. By aligning its product development efforts with these insights, the company launched a new line of drinks that became instant hits.

So, what does the future hold? The potential is limitless. As businesses continue to embrace data analytics, the boundaries of what's possible expand. The key to unlocking this potential lies in a curious and analytical mindset, coupled with a commitment to leveraging data ethically and responsibly.

Innovation and efficiency, once seen as separate pursuits, are now intertwined, with data as the binding thread. The path forward is clear: those who harness the power of data to inform their operations and innovation efforts will lead the next wave of business transformation.

Consider this: In an age where information is abundant, the ability to sift through noise to find actionable insights is more valuable than ever. Data analytics is not just a tool but a compass guiding businesses through the complexities of the modern world.

In conclusion, as we delve into the intricacies of operational efficiency and innovation, we see that data is not merely a backdrop but a catalyst. It drives decisions that streamline operations, ignites the spark of innovation, and, ultimately, shapes the future of businesses. The stories of companies leveraging data to achieve remarkable efficiencies and innovate boldly are just the beginning. The journey into the world of data analytics continues, promising new frontiers of knowledge and opportunity.

Case Studies of Data-Driven Decision-Making

A New Dawn in Healthcare: Revolutionizing Patient Care with Data

In the ever-evolving landscape of healthcare, a revolutionary change has been brewing, one that places data at the heart of patient care and treatment outcomes. Picture this: a hospital where every decision, from diagnosis to treatment plans, is informed by comprehensive data analytics. This is not a distant dream but a reality at a leading healthcare institution in the Midwest.

The Challenge: Personalizing Patient Care

The traditional one-size-fits-all approach to medicine has long been a stumbling block in achieving optimal patient outcomes. Every patient is unique, with their own genetic makeup, lifestyle, and health history. The challenge was clear: how could the hospital tailor treatments to the individual needs of each patient?

The Data Analytics Approach

The hospital embarked on an ambitious project to integrate data analytics into every facet of patient care. By analyzing vast amounts of medical data, including patient records, genetic information, and treatment outcomes, the hospital developed predictive models that could guide doctors in making personalized treatment decisions.

Imagine the power of knowing, with a high degree of certainty, how a patient might respond to a particular treatment based on similar cases and outcomes. This is precision medicine, enabled by data.

The Outcomes: A Leap Forward in Patient Care

The results were nothing short of extraordinary. Patients received treatments that were highly customized to their individual health profiles, leading to significantly improved outcomes. Recovery times shortened, and the rates of adverse reactions to medications plummeted.

But the impact didn't stop there. The hospital also saw a substantial reduction in healthcare costs, as treatments were more effective and required less trial and error. This case study serves as a beacon, illuminating the path for healthcare providers worldwide to follow suit.

Revolutionizing Retail: Predicting Consumer Trends with Precision

DATA DEMYSTIFIED: A BEGINNER'S GUIDE TO UNDERSTANDING THE WORLD THROUGH NUMBERS

Gone are the days when retailers relied solely on past sales data and gut instincts to predict future trends. In today's fast-paced market, a leading fashion retailer has rewritten the rules of the game by harnessing the power of data analytics.

The Challenge: Staying Ahead of Consumer Trends

The fashion industry is notoriously fickle, with trends emerging and fading at a breakneck pace. The retailer faced the daunting task of predicting these trends accurately to stock the right products at the right time, avoiding overproduction and wastage.

The Data Analytics Approach

By analyzing social media patterns, search trends, and online purchase data, the retailer developed sophisticated algorithms capable of predicting future fashion trends with impressive accuracy. This data-driven approach allowed them to adjust their inventory in real-time, aligning closely with emerging consumer preferences.

The Outcomes: A Trendsetter in Retail

The retailer not only succeeded in reducing waste and unsold inventory but also became a trendsetter, often beating competitors to market with the latest styles. The company's reputation soared, as did its profits, demonstrating the transformative power of data in anticipating consumer needs.

Transportation Transformed: Optimizing Routes with Data

The logistics industry, with its complex web of transportation routes and schedules, presents an ideal case for data-driven optimization.

The Challenge: Streamlining Logistics

A global shipping company faced significant challenges in optimizing its delivery routes. With an ever-changing landscape of traffic patterns, weather conditions, and shipping volumes, how could they ensure timely deliveries while minimizing fuel consumption?

The Data Analytics Approach

The company turned to data analytics, utilizing real-time traffic and weather data, along with historical shipping patterns, to dynamically optimize delivery routes. This approach allowed for on-the-fly adjustments, ensuring the most efficient path was always taken.

The Outcomes: A New Era in Logistics

The benefits were immediately apparent. Delivery times improved, customer satisfaction soared, and fuel consumption dropped significantly, leading to cost savings and a reduced environmental footprint. This case study is a testament to the power of data in transforming traditional industries, paving the way for a more efficient and sustainable future.

Each of these case studies showcases the transformative power of data across various industries. From healthcare to retail to logistics, the common thread is clear: data-driven decision-making not only leads to improved outcomes and efficiencies but also opens up new possibilities for innovation and service excellence.

The question then becomes, what future advancements will data unlock next? As we stand on the brink of this new data-driven era, the possibilities are as vast as the data itself.

Ethical Business Practices and Data

In the realm of modern business, data not only fuels innovation but also serves as the cornerstone of decision-making processes. Yet, as we navigate through this vast ocean of information, ethical considerations loom large on the horizon, casting shadows of doubt and concern. How do we harness the power of data while ensuring consumer privacy, data security, and mitigating algorithmic bias? These questions are not mere afterthoughts but central to building a trustworthy relationship with customers and stakeholders.

Consumer Privacy: A Sacred Trust

Imagine living in a world where every click, every purchase, and even every pause is monitored, analyzed, and stored. This is not the plot of a dystopian novel but the reality of the digital age. Consumer privacy has emerged as a pivotal concern, with individuals growing increasingly wary of how their personal information is used. Businesses face the challenge of balancing data collection for enhancing services and respecting the privacy of their users.

Transparency becomes the beacon guiding this delicate balance. By openly communicating what data is collected and for what purpose, businesses can demystify the process for consumers. It's about creating an environment where customers feel informed and in control of their personal information. This approach not only builds trust but also fosters a sense of partnership between the consumer and the company.

Data Security: Fortifying the Digital Fortress

With great data comes great responsibility. As businesses collect and store vast amounts of information, the specter of data breaches looms large. A single breach can shatter trust, tarnish reputations, and have financial ramifications. Therefore, securing data is not merely an IT concern but a fundamental business imperative.

Imagine your business as a fortress. Would you leave the gates open and unguarded? Certainly not. Data security involves layering defenses, from encryption to regular security audits, ensuring that customer data is protected against cyber threats. It's about being proactive, not reactive, in the face of evolving security challenges.

Algorithmic Bias: The Invisible Hand

Algorithms, those intricate formulas that sort, predict, and decide, have become the unseen arbiters of the digital age. However, they are not impervious to bias. Without careful oversight, algorithms can perpetuate and even amplify biases present in their training data, leading to unfair outcomes.

Addressing algorithmic bias requires a commitment to fairness and equity. It begins with the diversification of data sets, ensuring they reflect a broad spectrum of humanity. Moreover, regular audits of algorithmic decisions can uncover biases, making it possible to adjust and refine these digital decision-makers. It's about striving for algorithms that are not only intelligent but also equitable.

Navigating Ethical Dilemmas: Steering the Ship with Integrity

Confronting these ethical challenges head-on is daunting but not insurmountable. It requires a steadfast commitment to ethical principles, guiding businesses through the murky waters of the digital age.

- is not just a policy but a practice, involving clear communication and openness about data practices.

- means taking ownership of both the benefits and the risks of data, standing ready to address any issues that arise.

- is the compass that ensures businesses do not lose their way. Regulations such as GDPR and CCPA are not hurdles but guidelines toward ethical data usage.

But how do businesses build trust through responsible data practices? It starts with a culture that values ethics as much as it does innovation. From the boardroom to the development team, every decision must be weighed against its ethical implications.

Consider the story of a small startup that made transparency its cornerstone. By allowing customers to easily see and control the data collected about them, the startup not only complied with data protection regulations but also built a loyal customer base. Their commitment to ethical practices became their strongest selling point, distinguishing them in a crowded marketplace.

In Conclusion: The Path Forward

The journey toward ethical data practices is ongoing, marked by continuous learning and adaptation. As businesses, we hold the power to shape a world where data serves humanity, not the other way around. It's a world where privacy is respected, security is paramount, and fairness is non-negotiable.

Ethical business practices and data are not at odds but can coexist, creating a synergy that drives innovation while upholding our shared values. The path forward is clear, illuminated by the principles of transparency, accountability, and adherence to regulations. It's a path that leads to a future where businesses not only succeed but also contribute to a fairer, more secure digital world.

This vision of the future is not just aspirational but achievable. It requires courage, commitment, and collaboration. As we chart this course together, let us remember that in the realm of data, ethics is not a constraint but a catalyst for true innovation and lasting success.

Let's not just demystify data; let's dignify it with our ethical practices.

The Future of Data in Business

The landscape of business is undergoing a seismic shift, with data at its epicenter. As we stand on the brink of this transformation, it is imperative to cast our gaze forward, to the future where data not only informs but shapes our professional lives. This future is not a distant reality but an imminent evolution, marked by the burgeoning role of artificial intelligence (AI) and machine learning (ML), the rise of data marketplaces, and the ever-changing realm of data regulation. Each of these trends carries the potential to redefine the business world as we know it.

The Rise of AI and ML in Decision-Making

In the heart of this transformation lies the increasing reliance on AI and ML. Imagine a world where decisions, once the sole province of human intuition and experience, are now augmented by algorithms capable of analyzing vast datasets in mere seconds. This is not mere speculation but a reality unfolding before our eyes. AI and ML are not just tools but partners in the decision-making process, offering insights derived from patterns invisible to the human eye.

Yet, with great power comes great responsibility. As AI and ML take on more significant roles, the question of ethical AI usage becomes paramount. How do we ensure that these algorithms are free from bias, transparent in their workings, and respectful of privacy? The answer lies in rigorous ethical standards and continuous oversight—an ongoing dialogue between technology and humanity.

The Growth of Data Marketplaces

Another significant trend reshaping the business landscape is the emergence of data marketplaces. Picture these marketplaces as bustling digital bazaars, where data is the currency of choice. Companies can buy, sell, or trade data, unlocking new opportunities for innovation and customization. However, this new frontier also raises critical questions about data ownership, privacy, and consent. Navigating these marketplaces will require a nuanced understanding of both technology and ethics—a balancing act between leveraging data and respecting individual rights.

The Evolving Landscape of Data Regulation

As the role of data in business expands, so too does the tapestry of regulations governing its use. The General Data Protection Regulation (GDPR) in Europe and the California Consumer Privacy Act (CCPA) in the United States are just the beginning. We stand at the threshold of a new era of data regulation, one that will likely see more stringent controls on data collection, usage, and sharing.

Businesses must stay agile, ready to adapt to these evolving regulations. Compliance should not be seen as a burden but as a badge of honor—a testament to a company's commitment to ethical data practices.

Preparing for the Future

So, how can professionals prepare for this ever-evolving data landscape? The first step is education. Understanding the basics of AI and ML, familiarizing oneself with the intricacies of data marketplaces, and staying abreast of regulatory changes are essential. But knowledge alone is not enough. It requires a mindset shift—a willingness to embrace change, to question the status quo, and to think ethically about the implications of data usage.

In this journey toward the future, continuous learning and adaptability are your most valuable allies. The path may be fraught with challenges, but it is also ripe with opportunities—opportunities to innovate, to lead, and to shape the future of business in a data-driven world.

Let us ponder a question: Are we ready to navigate this future, to harness the power of data while upholding our ethical standards? The answer lies within each of us, in our willingness to embrace change, to learn, and to lead with integrity.

The future of data in business is not a distant dream but an unfolding reality. As we step into this new era, let us do so with a commitment to ethical practices, a passion for innovation, and an unwavering dedication to shaping a world where data not only informs but also enriches our professional lives.

This is our journey. Let's embark on it together.

Data in Healthcare

Revolutionizing Healthcare With Data

In the vast and intricate world of healthcare, a revolution is unfolding, one that is reshaping how care is delivered, decisions are made, and outcomes are improved. This transformation is driven by data, the lifeblood of modern medicine, pulsating through the industry and breathing new life into every aspect of patient care and public health strategy. Imagine, if you will, a future where treatments are not just based on general medical knowledge but are intricately tailored to each individual's genetic makeup, lifestyle, and even their preferences. This is not a distant dream but a rapidly approaching reality, thanks to the power of data analytics in healthcare.

The dawn of personalized medicine is upon us. It heralds a new era where each patient's unique data footprint guides the crafting of bespoke treatment plans, significantly boosting the effectiveness of medical interventions. But how does this monumental shift come to be? Through the meticulous analysis of vast amounts of patient data, from genetic information to lifestyle patterns, healthcare professionals can now identify the most effective treatments for each individual. This precision not only enhances patient outcomes but also optimizes resource allocation, ensuring that the right treatments get to the right people at the right time.

Central to this data-driven transformation is the adoption of electronic health records (EHRs). These digital repositories consolidate all patient information, providing a comprehensive view of an individual's health history at the click of a button. The impact? Enhanced care coordination, improved efficiency, and a significant reduction in medical errors. EHRs serve as the backbone of data analytics in healthcare, enabling the seamless aggregation, analysis, and exchange of vital health information.

But what does this mean for the patient, the healthcare provider, and the broader public health landscape?

For patients, the implications are profound. No longer mere passive recipients of care, they are now active participants in their health journey, armed with data that empowers them to make informed decisions about their treatments and lifestyle. The era of one-size-fits-all medicine is fading, giving way to an approach that recognizes and respects the individuality of each patient.

Healthcare providers, too, stand to benefit immensely from this data revolution. With access to a wealth of information at their fingertips, they can make more informed decisions, anticipate potential complications, and provide care that is both more effective and more efficient. The result? A significant enhancement in the quality of care, coupled with an increase in patient satisfaction.

On a broader scale, the integration of data analytics into public health strategies offers the potential to transform how we approach health and disease on a societal level. By analyzing trends and patterns within large datasets, public health officials can identify emerging health threats, track the spread of diseases, and allocate resources more effectively. This not only aids in the prevention and control of health crises but also paves the way for more targeted and effective public health campaigns.

Yet, as with any revolution, challenges abound. The ethical considerations of handling sensitive patient data, the need for robust data security measures, and the potential for widening health disparities if access to these technologies is unequal are just a few of the hurdles that must be overcome. Nevertheless, the potential benefits of this data-driven approach to healthcare are too significant to ignore.

Imagine a world where every treatment is optimized for the individual, where healthcare providers have all the information they need at their fingertips, and where public health strategies are informed by real-world data. This is not a mere fantasy but a future that is within our grasp, thanks to the revolutionary power of data in healthcare.

In the end, one truth remains clear: in the quest to improve healthcare outcomes, data is not just a tool; it is the key to unlocking a future where personalized, efficient, and effective care is not the exception but the norm. As we stand on the brink of this new era, one cannot help but wonder: what other transformations will the data revolution bring? Only time will tell, but one thing is certain—the future of healthcare is bright, and it is data-driven.

Predictive Analytics in Patient Care

Venturing deeper into the realm of healthcare, we find ourselves at the cusp of a significant evolution, one that is founded on the predictive capabilities of analytics. This chapter delves into the transformative power of predictive analytics in patient care, unraveling how historical patient data becomes the crystal ball through which future health events can be foreseen. The applications are vast and varied, from risk scoring for chronic diseases to predicting hospital readmission rates and optimizing the allocation of healthcare resources. Through vivid case studies, we will explore the successful implementations of these applications and their profound impact on patient outcomes.

Why does predictive analytics hold such promise for healthcare? The answer lies in its ability to sift through mountains of data, identifying patterns and trends that the human eye could never discern. This capacity for deep analysis enables healthcare providers to anticipate health issues before they manifest, offering a window of opportunity for early intervention and preventive strategies.

Consider the case of chronic disease management. Chronic diseases, such as diabetes and heart disease, are among the leading causes of death worldwide. Predictive analytics can revolutionize the management of these conditions by employing risk scoring systems. These systems analyze a patient's historical health data, lifestyle choices, and even genetic predispositions to calculate their risk of developing certain conditions. Armed with this information, healthcare providers can tailor interventions that preempt the onset of disease or mitigate its severity.

Hospital readmissions are another area where predictive analytics is making waves. Hospitals face significant penalties for high rates of readmission, not to mention the impact on patient health and satisfaction. By analyzing data from previous admissions, predictive models can identify patients who are at high risk of returning to the hospital. This insight allows for targeted post-discharge care plans designed to keep patients healthy and out of the hospital.

Resource allocation within healthcare facilities is yet another challenge addressed by predictive analytics. Hospitals must constantly juggle limited resources, from staffing to bed availability, while ensuring optimal patient care. Predictive models can forecast patient inflow, enabling administrators to allocate resources more effectively and efficiently, thus reducing wait times and improving patient care quality.

But how does all this come to life? Let's look at a real-world example. A hospital in the United States implemented a predictive analytics program to identify patients at high risk of sepsis, a life-threatening response to infection. By analyzing real-time data from electronic health records (EHRs), the system could alert healthcare providers of early signs of sepsis, allowing for rapid intervention. The result? A significant reduction in sepsis-related mortality rates.

This success story is but one of many illustrating the profound impact of predictive analytics on patient outcomes. But it's not without its challenges. Concerns around data privacy, the accuracy of predictions, and the need for healthcare providers to adapt to new technologies are valid and require careful consideration.

However, the potential benefits cannot be overstated. Predictive analytics offers a proactive approach to healthcare, shifting the paradigm from reactive to preventive. It empowers healthcare providers with actionable insights, enabling them to deliver care that is not only more effective but also more personalized.

Imagine a future where your health journey is mapped out with precision, where interventions are timely and tailored to your unique needs. This is not a distant dream but a reality being forged today through the power of predictive analytics in patient care.

As we conclude this chapter, one cannot help but ponder: What other innovations will predictive analytics inspire? How will it continue to reshape the landscape of healthcare? The possibilities are as vast as the data itself, and the journey ahead is filled with promise.

The future of healthcare is predictive, personalized, and powered by data. And as we stand on the threshold of this new era, we embrace the dawn of a health revolution, where the focus shifts from treating illness to preventing it, ensuring a healthier tomorrow for all.

Big Data's Role in Epidemic and Disease Control

In the labyrinth of modern healthcare, big data emerges as a beacon of hope, particularly in the realm of epidemic and disease control. This chapter illuminates how the colossus of data, when harnessed effectively, becomes an indispensable ally in the battle against infectious diseases. The stakes? Human lives and the stability of societies worldwide.

Imagine the world as a vast network, pulsating with information from countless sources: social media posts hinting at emerging health trends, travel records painting pictures of potential disease pathways, and healthcare reports providing real-time insights into population health. In the face of an outbreak, this myriad of data points coalesces into a formidable tool for epidemiologists and public health officials. The mission? To track, predict, and ultimately control the spread of diseases.

But how does this process unfold in the real world? Let's delve into the mechanics of big data analytics and its application during public health crises, with a spotlight on the COVID-19 pandemic—a stark exemplar of data's potential to guide global response efforts.

At the heart of big data's utility is its ability to offer real-time surveillance. As the novel coronavirus began its stealthy spread, researchers and public health authorities turned to unconventional data streams for early warning signs. Social media platforms, brimming with personal health anecdotes and concerns, became unexpected sentinels. An uptick in posts about fever or loss of smell in a specific area, for instance, could signal a brewing outbreak. This information, though seemingly trivial on the surface, fed into sophisticated algorithms designed to detect potential threats.

Travel records, too, played a pivotal role. By analyzing flight and passenger data, scientists could trace the virus's pathways, anticipating its next moves. This data-driven approach enabled countries to implement timely travel restrictions, aiming to curb the virus's spread.

Perhaps the most traditional yet crucial data source in this ensemble is healthcare reports. Hospitals and clinics across the globe contributed to a constant stream of data on case numbers, hospitalizations, and outcomes. This information, aggregated and analyzed, provided a clear picture of the pandemic's trajectory, informing both immediate response measures and long-term policy decisions.

One of the most compelling real-world examples of big data's prowess in managing public health crises is the development of COVID-19 dashboards. These interactive platforms synthesized data from diverse sources, offering an up-to-the-minute overview of the pandemic's status. Johns Hopkins University's COVID-19 dashboard, for instance, became an indispensable resource for both the public and policymakers, illustrating the power of data visualization in making complex information accessible.

In a world where speed can save lives, the ability to analyze data in real time is nothing short of revolutionary. Predictive modeling, a cornerstone of big data analytics, allowed for the forecasting of case surges, hospital needs, and the potential impact of public health interventions. These models, while not perfect, provided a crucial foundation for decision-making in an uncertain and rapidly evolving situation.

Yet, the story of big data in epidemic and disease control is not without its challenges. Concerns over privacy, data accuracy, and the digital divide remind us that the path forward requires careful navigation. The question of how to balance individual privacy with public health needs emerged as a central dilemma, sparking debates around the globe. Furthermore, the reliance on digital data inherently excludes those without access to technology, potentially skewing data and leaving vulnerable populations in the shadows.

Despite these hurdles, the potential of big data in managing public health crises remains vast and largely untapped. As we look to the future, the integration of artificial intelligence and machine learning promises to further enhance our ability to predict and control outbreaks. The lessons learned from the COVID-19 pandemic underscore the critical role of data in shaping effective, evidence-based responses.

Imagine a future where outbreaks are contained before they can become pandemics, where public health decisions are guided by a deep understanding of disease dynamics, and where the global community is united in its response to health threats. This is the promise of big data in epidemic and disease control—a promise that, with careful stewardship, holds the potential to transform our approach to public health.

As this chapter closes, we stand at the threshold of a new era in epidemic and disease control. Armed with data, driven by innovation, and guided by the principle of equity, we embark on a journey toward a healthier, more resilient world. The power of numbers, it seems, extends far beyond the abstract, reaching into the very fabric of our collective well-being. In the realm of public health, big data is not just a tool; it is a beacon of hope, lighting the way forward in our perennial battle against disease.

Ethical Considerations and Privacy Concerns

In the evolving landscape of healthcare, the sanctity of patient data emerges as a critical frontier, demanding our vigilant attention and ethical rigor. This chapter delves into the intricate web of ethical considerations and privacy concerns that underpin the collection, storage, and analysis of healthcare data. The stakes are high, for at the heart of this discussion lies the trust and safety of individuals whose personal health information (PHI) is both invaluable and vulnerable.

Healthcare data, with its deeply personal and sensitive nature, sits at the intersection of innovation and privacy. The imperative to protect this data cannot be overstated, especially in an era where breaches not only compromise individual privacy but also erode public trust in healthcare systems. But what does it truly take to safeguard such information in the digital age?

At the core of protecting PHI is the principle of patient consent. This fundamental right empowers individuals, granting them control over their own health information. Consent is not a mere formality but a profound exercise of autonomy and respect. It involves informing patients about what data is collected, how it will be used, and with whom it may be shared. Yet, obtaining consent is a nuanced process, requiring clear communication and an understanding of the patient's perspective. How do we ensure that consent is not only informed but also freely given in an environment that can be intimidating or confusing for patients?

Beyond consent, the anonymization of data presents itself as a critical tool in the quest to use health information responsibly. Anonymization strips away identifiers, transforming data into a format where individuals are no longer recognizable. This process, however, is fraught with challenges. The very techniques that protect privacy can, if not meticulously applied, lead to the loss of valuable information, potentially diminishing the data's utility for research and public health efforts. Moreover, in an age where vast datasets can be cross-referenced, the risk of re-identification looms large. The question then arises: how do we balance the benefits of data use with the imperative to protect individual identities?

Robust security measures are the bulwark against unauthorized access and breaches. Encryption, access controls, and continuous monitoring form the triad of a comprehensive security strategy. Imagine a fortress, not of stone and mortar, but of algorithms and protocols, designed to shield sensitive information from the prying eyes of cyber attackers. Yet, as technology advances, so too do the tactics of those with malicious intent. In this constant game of cat and mouse, vigilance and innovation in cybersecurity are paramount. Can we stay one step ahead of the threats, or is the risk of a breach an inevitable shadow over the digital landscape of healthcare?

Legal frameworks like the Health Insurance Portability and Accountability Act (HIPAA) in the United States serve as the scaffolding for the ethical use and protection of healthcare data. HIPAA, with its Privacy and Security Rules, lays down the law, dictating how PHI must be handled. Compliance with such regulations is not merely a legal obligation but a moral one, underscoring the commitment of healthcare providers to their patients' privacy and trust. Yet, the legal landscape is as complex as it is varied, with regulations differing across borders and jurisdictions. This patchwork of laws presents a formidable challenge for global health initiatives and research collaborations. How do we navigate this legal labyrinth to foster innovation while upholding the highest standards of privacy and ethics?

The implications of these ethical and privacy considerations extend far into the realm of healthcare delivery and patient care. Trust, once eroded, is not easily restored. A breach or misuse of data can lead to a reluctance among individuals to share their information, hindering not only their own care but also the broader efforts to improve public health and combat diseases.

In light of these challenges, the path forward is one of balance and vigilance. We must tread carefully, respecting the privacy and autonomy of individuals while harnessing the transformative potential of healthcare data. It is a journey fraught with complexity, but also ripe with opportunity—to redefine healthcare in the digital age, to build systems that are not only effective but also ethical and secure.

As we venture into this uncharted territory, let us carry with us a sense of responsibility and a commitment to the principles that guide ethical healthcare: respect for persons, beneficence, and justice. In doing so, we not only protect the privacy and dignity of individuals but also pave the way for a future where healthcare is informed by data, driven by compassion, and dedicated to the well-being of all.

The conversations around data ethics and privacy are far from over. They are evolving, just as rapidly as the technologies that spark them. It is our collective responsibility to engage in these discussions, to ask the hard questions, and to seek answers that respect both individual rights and the common good.

Innovations and Future Trends in Health Data

As we pivot from the ethical bedrock that must underpin the handling of healthcare data, we venture into a realm brimming with innovations and boundless possibilities. The horizon of healthcare is being redrawn by advancements in genomics, wearable health technologies, and AI-driven diagnostics. Each of these frontiers carries the promise to revolutionize patient care, presenting a mosaic of challenges and opportunities. The journey into this future is not just about embracing new technologies; it's about preparing for a paradigm shift in how we understand and interact with health data.

Genomics, the study of an individual's genes, is unraveling mysteries that have long eluded humanity. Imagine a world where your genetic makeup could predict potential health issues and guide personalized treatment plans. This is not the stuff of science fiction. Cutting-edge research in genomics is enabling just that, offering a glimpse into a future where diseases could be intercepted before they manifest. However, the road to this future is paved with complexities. The sheer volume and intricacy of genomic data demand a skilled workforce adept in not just understanding but also interpreting this information. The question then arises: Are we ready to educate and equip the next generation of healthcare professionals with these skills?

Wearable health technologies have woven themselves into the fabric of daily life, transforming the way we monitor our health. From fitness trackers to smartwatches, these devices collect a wealth of data, offering insights into our heart rate, sleep patterns, and activity levels. The potential of wearable technologies extends far beyond personal fitness. They hold the promise of enabling real-time monitoring of patients, potentially predicting and averting health crises. The vivid imagery of a future where your watch alerts you to a potential heart issue before it happens is becoming increasingly realistic. Yet, this future also demands a reevaluation of how we manage and protect this influx of personal health data. The challenge lies not just in collecting data but in ensuring its security and privacy.

The advent of AI-driven diagnostics heralds a new era in healthcare. Artificial intelligence, with its ability to learn and adapt, is poised to transform diagnostics by identifying patterns and anomalies that may elude the human eye. The implications for patient care are profound, offering the potential for early detection of diseases with greater accuracy. Yet, as we stand on the cusp of this revolution, we must ask ourselves: How do we ensure the ethical use of AI in healthcare? The opportunity to enhance diagnostics is immense, but so is the responsibility to use these technologies in a manner that respects patient autonomy and privacy.

The integration of genomics, wearable technologies, and AI-driven diagnostics into healthcare is not without its hurdles. One of the most pressing challenges is the need for a skilled workforce. The complexity of health data has escalated, and with it, the demand for professionals who can navigate this landscape. The future of healthcare will be shaped by those who can interpret vast datasets, discern patterns, and extract meaningful insights. This necessitates a paradigm shift in education and training, one that fosters interdisciplinary skills ranging from data science to bioethics.

Moreover, the potential for even more personalized patient care that these innovations offer is tantalizing. The ability to tailor treatments to the individual, informed by their genetic makeup, lifestyle, and real-time health data, could usher in a new era of medicine. This vision of personalized care is not merely about treating diseases; it's about preempting them, offering a roadmap to a healthier life tailored to each person's unique profile.

Yet, the path to personalized care is fraught with ethical considerations. How do we balance the benefits of personalized medicine with the need to protect individual privacy? The collection and analysis of health data on such an intimate level demand stringent safeguards and a renewed commitment to the ethical principles that guide patient care.

In conclusion, the future of healthcare data is a kaleidoscope of innovation, challenges, and opportunities. The advancements in genomics, wearable health technologies, and AI-driven diagnostics promise to redefine patient care, making it more personalized, predictive, and preemptive. However, realizing this future requires not just technological prowess but a commitment to ethical stewardship of health data, a skilled workforce capable of interpreting complex information, and a healthcare system that prioritizes patient privacy and autonomy. As we stand on the brink of this new era, let us embrace the opportunities while steadfastly addressing the challenges. The journey ahead is not just about the evolution of healthcare; it's about revolutionizing the very essence of patient care in the digital age.

Data in Education

Enhancing Learning Through Data Analytics

In the vast, interconnected web of the modern education sector, data analytics emerges as a beacon of innovation, transforming traditional teaching methodologies and fostering environments where personalized learning thrives. Imagine a classroom not as a one-size-fits-all space but as a dynamic ecosystem, tailored to the unique needs, pace, and interests of each student. This vision is no longer confined to the realm of imagination. Thanks to data analytics, it's becoming an achievable reality.

Gone are the days when teaching was a mere transmission of knowledge from educator to student, a process as impersonal as it was ineffective for many learners. In its place, data analytics ushers in an era of personalized education, a nuanced understanding of student engagement, and significantly enhanced educational outcomes. But how does this transformative process unfold?

At the heart of this evolution lies the integration of Learning Management Systems (LMS). These sophisticated platforms track a student's journey through the educational landscape, capturing every click, every submission, and every interaction. Far from being mere repositories of grades and attendance records, LMSs are the backbone of a data-driven approach to education. They adapt to a student's learning pace, identify areas of strength and weakness, and provide educators with actionable insights.

Consider the case of a student who struggles with math. Traditional teaching methods might see this student falling further behind, lost in a one-paced-fits-all approach. Enter data analytics. Through the LMS, educators can see precisely where the student's understanding starts to waver. Is it long division? Algebraic expressions? With this knowledge, the system can provide targeted exercises to bolster the student's understanding, adapting in real time to their pace of learning.

DATA DEMYSTIFIED: A BEGINNER'S GUIDE TO UNDERSTANDING THE WORLD THROUGH NUMBERS

But the impact of data analytics extends far beyond personalized learning paths. It revolutionizes student engagement. Interactive dashboards vividly display a student's progress, gamifying the learning experience. Suddenly, learning isn't just about getting through the next chapter of a textbook; it's about completing a quest, unlocking achievements, and witnessing personal growth in real time.

Can you envision a classroom where every student feels seen, understood, and supported? Data analytics makes this possible.

In one striking example, a high school in the Midwest implemented an LMS that leveraged data analytics to track student engagement. The results were illuminating. Educators discovered that students engaged most with materials that included interactive elements and real-world applications. This insight led to a significant overhaul of their teaching materials, making them more relevant and engaging for students. The outcome? Increased attendance, higher engagement, and improved grades.

However, the power of data analytics in education isn't confined to enhancing the student experience. It extends to educators, providing them with a treasure trove of insights. Through the analysis of data, teachers can refine their teaching strategies, ensuring they meet the needs of their diverse student body. Furthermore, this data can highlight trends and patterns that might go unnoticed, enabling educators to intervene early and effectively when students show signs of struggle or disengagement.

Yet, amidst this technological revolution, a question arises: Are we prepared to navigate the ethical considerations that accompany the use of data analytics in education? The collection and analysis of student data must be approached with the utmost care, ensuring privacy and security are never compromised.

It's a delicate balance, but one worth striving for. After all, the potential benefits of data analytics in education are profound.

Imagine a future where every student, regardless of background or learning style, has access to a personalized education that not only engages but inspires.

This is the promise of data analytics in the education sector—a promise that, with thoughtful implementation, can lead to a brighter future for all learners.

As we stand on the brink of this exciting frontier, let us embrace the possibilities that data analytics offers. Let's transform our educational systems, one data point at a time.

The revolution is here. Are we ready to be a part of it?

Data-Driven Decision-Making in Educational Institutions

Data-driven decision-making in educational institutions represents not just a shift but a seismic transformation in how schools and higher education entities approach every aspect of student education and resource management. This chapter delves into the pivotal role of data in steering strategic decisions that foster more efficient administration and elevate the quality of education provided.

The significance of data transcends mere numbers on a page; it encapsulates a story, a narrative that, when correctly interpreted, can guide institutions through the labyrinth of curriculum development, resource allocation, and policy decisions. But how, you might wonder, does this translation from data to decision manifest within the walls of an educational institution?

Consider the journey of curriculum development. Historically, curricula were often static, rarely deviating year to year, and heavily reliant on textbooks and materials that could quickly become outdated. In the current era, where information evolves at an unprecedented pace, this approach is no longer viable. Schools and universities now turn to data analytics to ensure their curricula remain relevant and engaging. By analyzing trends in student performance, feedback on course materials, and the evolving demands of the job market, educators can tailor their curricula to better prepare students for the challenges of tomorrow.

Imagine a world where every textbook chapter, every assignment, and every class discussion is aligned not only with educational standards but also with real-world applications that students are likely to encounter. This isn't a pipe dream; it's the direction in which data-driven curriculum development is steering education.

But the influence of data extends beyond the classroom walls. It plays a crucial role in resource allocation, ensuring that the finite resources of an institution are utilized where they can have the greatest impact. Through data analysis, schools can identify which programs yield the highest engagement and success rates and allocate funds accordingly. This ensures that investments are made not just in areas of existing strength but also in bolstering programs that are vital for student development yet may be underperforming.

Have you ever wondered why some schools seem to have an uncanny ability to introduce new programs or initiatives just as they're becoming relevant? It's not foresight; it's data analytics. By monitoring trends in enrollment and student interest, institutions can proactively adjust their offerings to meet evolving demands.

A particularly poignant example of this proactive adaptation can be seen in how institutions identify and respond to student needs. Through a detailed analysis of performance data, schools can pinpoint areas where students struggle and implement targeted interventions. This approach transforms the educational experience from a one-size-fits-all model to a personalized journey tailored to each student's needs.

But let's pause for a moment.

How can we ensure that the treasure trove of data available to educational institutions is used ethically and effectively? The answer lies in transparency, consent, and a steadfast commitment to using data to enhance, not hinder, the educational experience. By engaging with students, parents, and educators in an open dialogue about how data is used, institutions can build trust and ensure that their data-driven initiatives are met with support rather than skepticism.

In the realm of policy decisions, data acts as both a compass and a map, guiding institutions through the complex landscape of educational regulations and societal expectations. Policies informed by comprehensive data analysis can address pressing issues such as equity in education, student well-being, and the integration of technology in the classroom.

Consider the impact of a policy designed to improve digital literacy across a school district. By analyzing data on current levels of digital competency, access to technology, and performance in computer-based tasks, the district can craft a policy that not only addresses the gap in digital skills but also ensures that every student has the tools and support necessary to thrive in a digital world.

In conclusion, the role of data in educational institutions is both broad and deeply transformative. It informs decisions that touch every aspect of the educational process, from the macro level of policy formulation to the micro level of individual student support. As we continue to navigate the digital age, the integration of data analytics into educational decision-making processes is not just beneficial; it's essential.

By embracing a data-driven approach, educational institutions can ensure that they are not just keeping pace with the changing world but leading the charge towards a future where every student has the opportunity to succeed. The promise of data in education is vast, and its potential, when harnessed responsibly, is truly limitless.

Let this be our guiding principle: data, when used with intention and integrity, has the power to transform education for the better. Let's embark on this journey together, with eyes wide open to the possibilities that lie ahead.

Assessing and Improving Educational Outcomes

In the quest to decipher the intricate tapestry of educational success, a pivotal chapter unfolds, focusing on the assessment and improvement of educational outcomes. This journey delves deep into the heart of methodologies employed to scrutinize learning effectiveness, weaving through the realms of standardized testing, performance metrics, and qualitative assessments. The goal? To illuminate the path educators and administrators tread in utilizing data to foster enhancements, set ambitious goals, and measure the triumphs of their

DATA DEMYSTIFIED: A BEGINNER'S GUIDE TO UNDERSTANDING THE WORLD THROUGH NUMBERS

endeavors over time, all the while emphasizing the paramount importance of a continuous improvement cycle in education.

Embarking on this exploration, one might ask, "What tools lie at the core of assessing educational outcomes?" The answer emerges as a multifaceted mosaic of methodologies, each with its unique strengths and limitations.

Standardized testing, a cornerstone in this mosaic, offers a uniform measure of student achievement across diverse educational landscapes. Like a beacon casting light on the vast expanse of the sea, these tests aim to illuminate areas of proficiency and need within the student populace. However, the waters are not always calm; critics argue that the high stakes associated with such testing can sometimes obscure the true measure of learning, casting shadows over creativity and critical thinking.

Performance metrics, on the other hand, serve as navigational stars, guiding educators in their quest to evaluate and enhance teaching effectiveness. Through a detailed analysis of grades, attendance records, and participation rates, a picture emerges, revealing the intricate patterns of student engagement and achievement. This data, when harnessed correctly, can lead to targeted interventions that address the root causes of underperformance, much like a gardener tending to the needs of individual plants in a diverse ecosystem.

Stepping beyond the quantitative realm, qualitative assessments offer a kaleidoscope of insights into the learning process. Observations, interviews, and student portfolios open windows into the minds of learners, capturing the nuances of thought, the sparks of creativity, and the depth of understanding that numbers alone cannot convey. This rich tapestry of data paints a vivid picture of educational outcomes, inviting educators to delve deeper into the art and science of teaching.

With these tools in hand, educators and administrators embark on a journey of continuous improvement, a cycle that breathes life into the educational process. It begins with the collection of data, a careful gathering of insights from the field. This step is followed by analysis, a meticulous examination of data to uncover trends, challenges, and opportunities. The cycle progresses to implementation, where findings are translated into actionable strategies designed to enhance learning outcomes. And finally, evaluation, a reflective stage where the impact of these strategies is assessed, setting the stage for the cycle to begin anew.

Imagine a classroom where the cycle of improvement is in constant motion, where every lesson is informed by data, every strategy is evaluated for its impact, and every decision is guided by the goal of maximizing student success. This is not a distant dream but a tangible reality in schools that embrace the power of data in education.

In this dynamic landscape, the role of educators transcends traditional boundaries. They become gardeners, nurturing the growth of each student; navigators, steering the educational journey with precision; and alchemists, transforming raw data into gold—the gold of knowledge, insight, and improvement.

The journey does not end here. The quest for enhanced educational outcomes is a never-ending voyage, propelled by the winds of innovation and the currents of change. As we navigate these waters, let us hold fast to the belief that data, when wielded with wisdom and care, can illuminate the path to a brighter educational future.

In the words of the famed educator John Dewey, "Education is not preparation for life; education is life itself." Through the lens of data, we gain the clarity and insight needed to enrich this life, making every moment of learning an opportunity to grow, to improve, and to succeed.

Let this chapter serve as a beacon, guiding educators, administrators, and all stakeholders in the noble quest to demystify data and harness its power for the betterment of education. For in the numbers, in the patterns, and in the stories they tell, lies the key to unlocking the full potential of every learner.

And so, with eyes wide open to the possibilities, let us step forward into the light of understanding, armed with the tools of assessment and improvement, ready to shape the future of education—one data point at a time.

The Challenges of Data Privacy and Security in Education

In the evolving landscape of education, where data becomes the compass guiding decisions and strategies, a new chapter unfolds, addressing the paramount concerns of data privacy and security. This narrative ventures into the realm where numbers and personal stories intertwine, revealing the delicate balance between harnessing the power of data and protecting the sanctity of individual privacy.

At the heart of this dialogue lies the sensitivity of student data. Imagine, for a moment, the vast repositories of information held within the walls of educational institutions—academic records that narrate the journey of learning, personal information that whispers the tales of individual identities, and engagement data that reveals the patterns of student interactions. The richness of this data, while invaluable for educational advancement, casts a shadow of vulnerability, exposing students to risks if not safeguarded with the utmost care.

Why, one might ask, does this matter so profoundly? The answer echoes in the corridors of educational ethics: students, in their pursuit of knowledge, should not have to forfeit their right to privacy. Thus, the responsibility falls upon educational institutions to erect robust fortifications around this data, shielding it from unauthorized access and breaches.

Navigating this terrain requires a nuanced understanding of both the educational benefits derived from data and the potential perils that lurk when privacy is compromised. On one hand, data analytics offer a beacon of light, illuminating the paths to personalized education, early identification of learning challenges, and the optimization of curricular offerings. These insights, drawn from the depths of data, enable educators to tailor their approaches to meet the diverse needs of their students, crafting an educational experience that resonates with each learner's unique journey.

On the other hand, the specter of data breaches and unauthorized use casts a long shadow, raising alarms about the security of sensitive information. Stories abound, painting grim portraits of identity theft, manipulation of academic records, and the unauthorized sharing of personal information, all stemming from lapses in data security. Such breaches not only erode trust but also carry profound implications for the affected individuals, extending far beyond the confines of the classroom.

Enter the guardians of student privacy: legislation such as the Family Educational Rights and Privacy Act (FERPA) in the United States. Crafted with the intent of protecting student education records, FERPA serves as a bulwark against the indiscriminate sharing of information, ensuring that students and their families retain control over their educational data. Under its watchful eye, educational institutions are mandated to implement stringent data protection measures, a task that demands both vigilance and foresight.

Yet, the question remains: how do we strike the perfect balance? The answer lies not in the extremes but in the harmonious integration of data utility and privacy protection. It calls for a culture of data literacy, where all stakeholders understand the value of information and the importance of its safeguarding. It demands robust technological infrastructures, capable of thwarting cyber threats while facilitating the responsible use of data for educational enhancement. And, fundamentally, it requires a commitment to transparency, ensuring that students and their families are informed participants in the data ecosystem, empowered to make decisions about their information.

Consider, for a moment, an educational institution that embodies these principles. Here, data flows like a river, nourishing the landscape of education without eroding the banks of privacy. Teachers, equipped with insights drawn from secure data analyses, tailor their instruction to the needs of each student, fostering an environment where learning thrives. Students, confident in the security of their personal information, engage more fully, knowing that their privacy is respected and protected.

This is not a distant utopia but a reachable reality, one that demands our collective effort and commitment. As we navigate the complexities of data privacy and security in education, let us be guided by a shared vision: to harness the transformative power of data while upholding the sanctity of privacy. In this endeavor, let us remember that at the core of every data point lies a human story, deserving of our respect and protection.

And so, as we turn the page on this chapter, let us carry forward the lessons learned, embracing the challenges and opportunities that lie ahead. For in this delicate balance between data utility and privacy protection, we find the key to unlocking a future where education is both personalized and secure, where the potential of every learner is realized in an environment of trust and respect.

The journey continues, and with each step, we forge a path towards a brighter, more informed, and secure educational landscape.

Emerging Trends and Future Directions

As we peer into the horizon of educational innovation, a vista of emerging trends and future directions unfurls before us, promising a world where education is not just a matter of imparting knowledge but a dynamic ecosystem powered by data. The potential of artificial intelligence (AI) and machine learning (ML), the security promise of blockchain technology, and the transformative power of big data stand as pillars that could redefine educational landscapes. Yet, with great power comes great responsibility—the need to navigate these advancements while addressing ethical concerns has never been more crucial.

Imagine classrooms where AI and ML technologies act as personalized learning assistants, capable of adapting educational content to match the unique learning pace and style of each student. Such a future is not far off. In these classrooms, AI algorithms analyze students' performance in real-time, identifying strengths and weaknesses, and customizing learning materials accordingly. This personalized approach could revolutionize learning outcomes, making education more effective and inclusive. But how do we ensure that these AI systems are free from biases? How do we protect the privacy of the data they process?

Engaging the reader directly, what would you feel if an AI knew more about your learning habits than you do? The thought might be unsettling to some, highlighting the importance of ethical AI development. Developers and educators must work hand in hand to create AI systems that are transparent, explainable, and governed by ethical guidelines that protect students' privacy and autonomy.

Blockchain technology, often associated with cryptocurrencies, holds promising applications in securing educational records. With its decentralized and tamper-evident ledger, blockchain can provide a secure and unchangeable record of students' academic achievements. This could simplify the verification of academic credentials, reduce fraud, and enhance the mobility of students across global educational landscapes. Yet, the challenge lies in implementing such a system on a large scale, ensuring it is accessible and user-friendly for institutions, students, and employers alike.

Big data analytics, the practice of examining large datasets to uncover hidden patterns and correlations, offers unprecedented opportunities for system-wide educational reforms. Through the analysis of data from various sources, educators and policymakers can gain insights into the effectiveness of teaching methods, the allocation of resources, and the overall performance of educational systems. This could lead to more informed decisions that enhance the quality of education. However, the collection and use of big data raise significant privacy concerns. How do we balance the benefits of big data analytics with the need to protect individuals' privacy?

One-line paragraph for emphasis:

The dialogue between technology and education is ongoing, and it must be inclusive.

The opportunities presented by AI, blockchain, and big data are immense, but so are the challenges. As we venture further into this data-driven educational future, the dialogue among educators, policymakers, and technologists becomes increasingly vital. It is through this collaborative effort that we can harness the benefits of these advancements while addressing ethical concerns.

Moreover, integrating quotations or dialogues from experts in the field can enrich this discussion. For instance, a leading AI researcher might say, "The goal of AI in education is not to replace teachers but to augment their capabilities and to provide personalized learning experiences that were previously unimaginable." Such insights can offer a grounded perspective on the potential of these technologies.

In conclusion, the future of education through the lens of data and technology is bright but requires careful navigation. We stand at the precipice of a new era in education, one that promises personalized learning, secure and verifiable records, and data-driven reforms. Yet, as we embrace these advancements, we must remain vigilant, ensuring that ethical considerations and human values guide our journey. The path forward is not without its challenges, but with ongoing dialogue and collaboration, we can create an educational future that leverages the full potential of data while safeguarding the rights and dignity of all learners.

Thus, the narrative of 'Data Demystified: A Beginner's Guide to Understanding the World Through Numbers' does not end here but continues with each step we take towards a future where education is empowered by data, yet grounded in humanity.

Data in Governance and Public Policy

Leveraging Data for Effective Governance

In the digital age, data serves as the bedrock upon which the edifice of modern governance is constructed. Governments, from sprawling federal entities to local town councils, increasingly lean on the vast ocean of data at their disposal. This reliance is not without reason. Through the meticulous analysis of data, public officials can now make decisions that are not just informed but are also predictive, paving the way for a future where governance is both proactive and precisely tailored to meet the needs of its citizens.

Imagine a city where traffic jams are a relic of the past. Sensors embedded in roads and traffic lights feed real-time data into a central system. This system, leveraging the power of data analytics, adjusts signal timings on the fly, optimizing traffic flow. Such a scenario is not a flight of fancy but a tangible reality in some of the world's most forward-thinking cities. This transformation from reactive to predictive governance embodies the potential of data-driven decision-making.

But how do governments harness this potential? The journey begins with the collection of data - a process that has become increasingly sophisticated. From social media analytics to satellite imaging, the tools at the disposal of public administrations are both varied and powerful. However, the true challenge lies in the interpretation of this data. Here, the role of data scientists in governance becomes invaluable. By distilling complex datasets into actionable insights, they enable governments to allocate resources more efficiently, anticipate future trends, and engage with citizens in meaningful ways.

Consider the realm of public health. During health crises, such as the recent global pandemic, governments relied heavily on data to guide their responses. Tracking infection rates, hospital capacity, and vaccination progress allowed for dynamic adjustments to public health policies. This data-driven approach not only saved lives but also highlighted the indispensable role of data in managing public health emergencies.

Yet, the benefits of leveraging data for governance extend beyond crisis management. Open data initiatives, where governments make datasets publicly available, have fostered an unprecedented level of transparency. Citizens can now scrutinize government spending, understand policy decisions, and participate in governance in ways previously unimaginable. This openness has not only improved public services but has also built a bridge of trust between governments and the people they serve.

But what does this look like in practice? Take the city of Toronto, for example. Its Open Data portal allows citizens to access a wealth of information, from road closures to city budget data. This initiative has empowered residents, journalists, and civic activists to engage in informed dialogue with their government, leading to more responsive and accountable governance.

However, the path to data-driven governance is not without its pitfalls. Concerns over privacy and data security loom large, posing significant challenges. Moreover, the digital divide threatens to leave behind those without access to technology. Addressing these concerns is crucial for ensuring that the benefits of data-driven governance are equitably distributed.

So, where do we go from here? The future of governance lies in the hands of those who can skillfully navigate the vast seas of data. It requires a commitment to transparency, a dedication to equity, and a relentless pursuit of innovation.

For governments willing to embrace these principles, the possibilities are boundless. Imagine a world where policies are not just reactive but predictive, where public services are not just adequate but exceptional, and where citizen engagement is not just encouraged but amplified. This is the promise of data-driven governance.

In conclusion, the increasing reliance on data for effective governance is not just a trend but a paradigm shift. As we continue to demystify data, we unlock the potential to transform public administration, making governance more efficient, transparent, and inclusive. The journey is complex and fraught with challenges, but the destination—a world where data empowers both governments and citizens—is undoubtedly worth the effort.

Let us ask ourselves: Are we ready to navigate this brave new world of data-driven governance? The answer to this question will shape not just the future of governance but the very fabric of our societies.

Data-Driven Policy Making

In an era where the volume of data grows exponentially, the art and science of policy-making are undergoing a profound transformation. Data-driven policy-making emerges not just as a method but as a paradigm, promising a future where decisions are grounded in evidence rather than intuition or tradition. This chapter delves into the intricate process of data-driven policy-making, illuminating its role in sculpting policies that are not only effective but also equitable and forward-looking.

At the heart of data-driven policy-making lies the meticulous analysis of data to identify societal needs, predict the outcomes of various policy options, and monitor the effectiveness of implemented policies. This approach, when executed correctly, can lead to transformative changes across sectors, including urban planning, public health, and environmental protection, to name just a few.

Consider the challenge of urban sprawl, a critical issue facing many growing cities around the world. Traditional approaches often resulted in short-term solutions that failed to address underlying problems or anticipate future growth effectively. However, with the advent of data-driven urban planning, cities can now harness the power of geographic information systems (GIS), population data, and environmental impact assessments to design sustainable urban environments. These tools allow policymakers to visualize the potential outcomes of different development strategies, ensuring that growth is managed in a way that balances economic, social, and environmental concerns.

A compelling case study in this regard comes from Singapore, a city-state known for its meticulous urban planning. Through the use of data analytics, Singapore has been able to optimize its limited space to accommodate both its population's needs and its economic ambitions. The city's planners employ sophisticated models that simulate various scenarios, taking into account factors such as population growth, housing needs, and green space requirements. This approach has allowed Singapore to become a model of sustainable urban development, showcasing the potential of data-driven policy-making in creating livable, resilient cities.

Turning our attention to public health, the recent global pandemic underscored the critical importance of data in managing health crises. Governments and health organizations worldwide relied on a constant stream of data to make informed decisions regarding lockdowns, vaccination campaigns, and resource allocation. Data-driven models were instrumental in predicting the spread of the virus, identifying hotspots, and planning healthcare responses. The success stories are numerous, from countries that managed to flatten the curve to regions that efficiently rolled out vaccination programs, all underscored by the judicious use of data.

However, the journey toward data-driven policy-making is not without its challenges. Questions of privacy, ethical use of data, and the digital divide pose significant hurdles. Ensuring that data is used responsibly and that all members of society can benefit from its potential requires careful consideration and robust governance frameworks.

Furthermore, the successful implementation of data-driven policy-making depends on the availability of skilled professionals who can analyze and interpret data. Building capacity in this area is crucial for governments wishing to leverage the full potential of data-driven approaches.

The promise of data-driven policy-making is vast. It holds the key to more responsive, efficient, and effective governance. Yet, realizing this promise will require a concerted effort from all stakeholders involved, from policymakers and data scientists to citizens and the private sector.

In the face of growing complexity and rapidly changing societal needs, the question is no longer whether data should inform policy-making but how we can ensure it is done effectively and ethically. As we continue to navigate this data-rich world, the principles of transparency, inclusivity, and innovation must guide our path forward.

Let this be a call to action for policymakers, researchers, and citizens alike. The future of governance is data-driven, and the time to embrace this future is now. Together, we can harness the power of data to create policies that not only address the challenges of today but also pave the way for a brighter, more sustainable tomorrow.

In conclusion, data-driven policy-making is not just a tool but a transformative force that can redefine the landscape of governance. By embracing this approach, we can ensure that our policies are not just reactive but proactive, not just adequate but visionary. The journey ahead is filled with potential, and with data as our compass, we can navigate towards a future where informed, evidence-based decisions lead the way.

Challenges in Public Data Management

Managing public data presents a myriad of challenges and complexities, each layer more intricate than the last. From the initial stages of data collection to the final hurdles of ensuring accessibility, the journey is fraught with obstacles that can impede the utility and integrity of the information. These challenges are not mere technical issues but are deeply rooted in the very fabric of how data is perceived, handled, and governed.

Imagine a world where every piece of data, no matter how trivial it seems, holds the key to unlocking profound insights about our society. Yet, this treasure trove of information is often ensnared in a web of challenges. Data collection, for one, is a colossal task that navigates between the Scylla of comprehensiveness and the Charybdis of precision. How do we ensure that the data collected is both wide-ranging and accurate? This question lingers in the air, unanswered, as researchers and data managers grapple with the limitations of their tools and methodologies.

Moreover, the quality of data is a concern that cannot be overstated. In an era where "fake news" and misinformation are rampant, ensuring the veracity and reliability of public data is paramount. Yet, the path to high-quality data is beset with potholes of human error, biases in data collection methods, and the ever-present specter of data tampering. The integrity of data is the backbone of effective decision-making. Without it, are we not merely building castles on sand?

Accessibility, too, presents a significant hurdle. In the digital age, one might assume that accessing public data is as simple as a few clicks. However, the reality is far from this ideal. Vast swathes of valuable data are locked away behind paywalls, trapped in outdated formats, or buried in the depths of poorly designed databases. The question then arises: If data is not accessible to all, can it truly be considered public?

Integrating data from disparate sources is akin to assembling a jigsaw puzzle without the picture on the box as a guide. Each piece of data, from different domains and sectors, speaks its own language, follows its own rules. How do we then merge these pieces into a coherent whole? The barriers are not merely technical but also bureaucratic, as data often resides in siloed repositories guarded by different agencies with their own priorities and agendas.

Recognizing these challenges is but the first step. Overcoming them requires a concerted effort and a multifaceted approach. The adoption of advanced data management technologies holds promise. Artificial intelligence and machine learning algorithms offer powerful tools for cleaning, integrating, and analyzing vast datasets, making sense of the chaos. Yet, technology alone is not a panacea.

Inter-agency collaborations emerge as a beacon of hope in this complex landscape. By breaking down the silos and fostering a culture of data sharing and cooperation, we can begin to weave a tapestry of integrated data that is more than the sum of its parts. Such collaborations, however, demand robust data governance frameworks that prioritize data integrity, privacy, and ethical considerations.

Imagine a framework that not only ensures the quality and accessibility of data but also respects the privacy of individuals and the ethical implications of data use. This is not a distant dream but a necessary foundation for leveraging public data effectively. Establishing these frameworks is a Herculean task that requires the collaboration of policymakers, data managers, and the public.

Efforts to overcome these challenges are underway, with initiatives at various levels of government and the private sector working towards better data management practices. Yet, the road ahead is long and winding.

The journey of managing public data is fraught with challenges, but it is also filled with opportunities. Opportunities to transform how we understand and interact with the world through numbers. Opportunities to make data not just accessible but meaningful to everyone.

This chapter has peeled back the layers of complexity in public data management, revealing the challenges that lie beneath. Yet, it also shines a light on the path forward, a path paved with collaboration, innovation, and a steadfast commitment to integrity and accessibility.

Let us not shy away from these challenges. Instead, let us embrace them, for in doing so, we unlock the true potential of public data. A potential that can lead to a deeper understanding of our world and, ultimately, to better decisions that shape a brighter future for all.

In navigating the labyrinth of public data management, let us be guided by the principles of transparency, inclusiveness, and innovation. For it is only by confronting these challenges head-on that we can demystify the world of data and harness its power for the greater good.

Privacy, Security, and Ethical Considerations

In the realm of data, a delicate balance exists between the potential for public good and the protection of individual freedoms. As we delve deeper into the nuances of data usage, especially in governance and public policy, the specters of privacy, security, and ethical considerations loom large. This chapter aims to illuminate these critical concerns, offering insights into the complex interplay between leveraging data for societal benefits and safeguarding the rights and liberties of citizens.

Privacy, a fundamental right, often finds itself in the crosshairs of data utilization techniques. With the advent of sophisticated surveillance technologies and data analytics, the line between public safety and intrusive monitoring has become increasingly blurred. Picture a city, its streets lined with cameras, every movement tracked, and every action analyzed. Here, the imagery of Orwell's "1984" ceases to be fiction, morphing into a potential reality of modern surveillance. The question then arises: How do we navigate this tightrope, ensuring security without descending into a surveillance state?

Security concerns extend beyond the realm of surveillance, touching upon the integrity and protection of data itself. In an age where cyber-attacks are rampant, safeguarding sensitive information becomes paramount. Imagine the chaos that would ensue if personal data, from medical records to financial information, were to fall into the wrong hands. The consequences would be dire, eroding trust in institutions and potentially causing significant harm to individuals and communities.

Ethical considerations serve as the compass guiding the use of data. In the quest to utilize data for the public good, ethical dilemmas abound. Can data collected for one purpose be repurposed for another without consent? Is it ethical to use predictive analytics in law enforcement, potentially leading to profiling and discrimination? These questions demand careful contemplation. They underscore the need for an ethical framework that respects the dignity and rights of individuals, ensuring that data use benefits society without infringing on personal liberties.

The General Data Protection Regulation (GDPR) stands as a beacon, illuminating the path toward responsible data use. This regulatory framework underscores the importance of consent, data minimization, and the right to privacy. It serves as a testament to the possibility of harmonizing the benefits of data with the protection of individual rights. Yet, the GDPR is but one piece of the puzzle. Globally, the approaches to data privacy and security vary, highlighting the necessity for international cooperation and dialogue in crafting policies that transcend borders.

Consider the implications of data misuse in the context of law enforcement. The potential for predictive policing to prevent crime is tantalizing. Yet, without stringent ethical guidelines, such practices could lead to a dystopian reality where individuals are judged not by their actions but by algorithms' predictions. Here, the ethical quandary becomes stark: How do we harness the power of data to enhance security while ensuring that such technologies do not undermine the very fabric of justice and equality?

One-line paragraphs, like a lighthouse in a stormy sea, emphasize the core of our discourse: Data, in all its potential, carries with it a profound responsibility.

This chapter has ventured into the heart of the issues surrounding privacy, security, and ethics in data use. Through vivid imagery and probing questions, it has sought to unravel the complexities of these concerns. The balance between leveraging data for the public good and protecting individual freedoms is delicate, requiring constant vigilance and thoughtful consideration.

In navigating these waters, we must be guided by principles of transparency, accountability, and respect for individual rights. Only then can we ensure that the use of data, in all its forms, serves to uplift rather than oppress. The journey toward responsible data use is ongoing, fraught with challenges but also brimming with possibilities. Let us proceed with caution, but also with hope, for in the ethical use of data lies the potential to transform our world for the better.

As we close this chapter, let us remember: The power of data is immense, but so is our responsibility to use it wisely. In the intersection of privacy, security, and ethics, lies the future of our digital society. Let us tread carefully, but boldly, towards a future where data serves humanity, respecting our rights and enhancing our collective well-being.

The Future of Data in Public Sector Innovation

The horizon of public sector innovation glimmers with the promise of data-driven transformation. As we peer into the future, the integration of emerging technologies such as Artificial Intelligence (AI), blockchain, and the Internet of Things (IoT) in governance and public policy heralds a new epoch. These technologies, armed with the power of data, stand poised to revolutionize public administration, elevate citizen services, and ignite policy innovation. However, this bright future is not without its shadows. The digital

DATA DEMYSTIFIED: A BEGINNER'S GUIDE TO UNDERSTANDING THE WORLD THROUGH NUMBERS

literacy of policymakers and public administrators emerges as a critical fulcrum, balancing the promise of technological advances with the perils they pose.

Imagine a world where AI not only predicts public health crises but also devises preemptive strategies, saving countless lives. Visualize a government where blockchain ensures the integrity of public records, making corruption a relic of the past. Picture a city where IoT devices optimize energy consumption, creating a sustainable environment. These are not mere fantasies but tangible possibilities, provided we navigate the intricate dance of innovation with wisdom.

The potential of AI in public administration is boundless. From streamlining bureaucratic processes to enhancing decision-making with predictive analytics, AI could redefine the essence of governance. Yet, this marvel comes with its maze. The opacity of AI algorithms, the specter of bias, and the challenge of accountability loom large. Questions arise: How do we ensure AI serves the public interest without infringing on individual rights? Can we demystify AI's decision-making processes to maintain public trust?

Blockchain technology offers a beacon of transparency and security. By enabling decentralized and immutable record-keeping, blockchain can fortify the foundations of democracy. Elections could be transformed with blockchain, ensuring tamper-proof voting and instilling unwavering confidence in electoral processes. However, the path is strewn with hurdles. The complexity of blockchain technology and the scalability of such solutions demand keen attention. Moreover, the transition to blockchain-based systems necessitates a seismic shift in institutional structures and mindsets.

The proliferation of IoT devices in urban management and public services can usher in an era of unparalleled efficiency and sustainability. Smart cities, powered by IoT, can optimize resource use, reduce environmental footprints, and enhance the quality of life. Yet, this interconnectedness brings vulnerability. The security of IoT networks and the privacy of citizens become paramount concerns. How do we safeguard against cyber vulnerabilities that could paralyze a city? In what ways can we protect the privacy of individuals in an increasingly connected world?

The fulcrum upon which this technological transformation teeters is digital literacy. Policymakers and public administrators must possess the knowledge and skills to harness these technologies effectively. This requires a commitment to continuous learning and an openness to interdisciplinary collaboration. The complexity of emerging technologies demands not just technical expertise but also ethical discernment. As we tread into this new era, the cultivation of a digitally literate and ethically conscious public sector workforce becomes indispensable.

Moreover, the ethical dilemmas and risks associated with these technologies necessitate a robust framework. A framework that not only fosters innovation but also safeguards against misuse. It is imperative to strike a balance, ensuring that the pursuit of efficiency and transparency does not compromise ethical standards or citizen rights.

The journey ahead calls for courage and caution in equal measure. It beckons us to envision a future where technology and data serve as instruments of public good, enhancing governance, empowering citizens, and nurturing innovation. Yet, it also implores us to tread thoughtfully, recognizing the weight of our responsibility to use these tools wisely and ethically.

In closing, the future of data in public sector innovation is radiant with possibility. Emerging technologies, guided by the principles of transparency, accountability, and inclusivity, have the potential to redefine public service for the better. As we embark on this journey, let us harness the power of data and technology with wisdom and foresight. For in our hands lies not just the capability to transform governance but the opportunity to shape a future where technology uplifts humanity, fostering a world that is more just, more efficient, and more humane.

Let us not shy away from the challenges but embrace them as catalysts for growth and innovation. The future beckons with open arms. Will we answer the call?

Big Data and the Internet of Things (IoT)

Unpacking Big Data

In today's digital age, the term "big data" buzzes through conversations across industries, from tech-savvy startups to traditional institutions keen on innovation. But what exactly is big data, and why does it matter? Imagine standing beneath a waterfall, feeling the overwhelming force of water rushing over you – this is akin to the relentless, powerful flow of data in our modern world. Big data isn't just a larger version of the datasets we're used to; it's a whole new realm of complexity and opportunity.

At its core, big data is characterized by four key traits: volume, velocity, variety, and veracity. Each of these dimensions adds to the unique challenges and advantages that big data presents.

Volume, the first of these characteristics, refers to the sheer amount of data. Every day, billions of digital interactions occur, from tweets shared to transactions made on e-commerce platforms. This vast sea of data is far beyond what traditional databases can handle.

Next, velocity highlights the speed at which this data is generated and needs to be processed. Social media feeds update in real-time, financial markets fluctuate by the second, and climate sensors continuously stream new data. The rapid pace at which data flows requires equally swift analysis to be meaningful.

Variety speaks to the diverse sources and types of data available. From structured numbers and dates in databases to unstructured text in social media posts and video content, the range of data types adds layers of complexity to collection and analysis.

Lastly, veracity refers to the quality and reliability of data. With so much information available, ensuring accuracy and filtering out noise become paramount. Poor data quality can lead to misguided conclusions and decisions.

Consider the differences between traditional datasets and big data through the lens of an e-commerce platform. In the past, businesses might have tracked simple metrics like monthly sales or inventory levels. Today, they analyze vast arrays of data, from customer click patterns to real-time feedback on social media, to predict trends and personalize shopping experiences.

The challenges posed by big data are as vast as the opportunities. With the right tools and strategies, organizations can mine this wealth of information for insights that drive innovation and strategic decision-making. For instance, healthcare researchers use big data to predict disease patterns and improve patient outcomes. Retailers analyze shopping behaviors to tailor marketing strategies and enhance customer satisfaction.

But how do we navigate this complex landscape?

Firstly, robust data management systems are essential to handle the volume and velocity of data. These systems must not only store massive quantities of information but also provide the processing power to analyze it swiftly.

Equally important is the development of sophisticated algorithms capable of sifting through the variety of data types to find meaningful patterns. Machine learning and artificial intelligence play crucial roles here, learning from the data to make predictions and uncover insights that would be impossible for humans to find on their own.

Veracity, however, demands a human touch. Ensuring data quality and reliability requires vigilant oversight and constant refinement of data collection and analysis processes. This is where data scientists and analysts become invaluable, blending technical skills with critical thinking to separate signal from noise.

And yet, as we stand at the brink of this data-driven frontier, ethical considerations loom large. With great power comes great responsibility. The ability to collect and analyze vast amounts of data raises questions about privacy, consent, and data security.

How do we balance the benefits of big data with the need to protect individual rights?

This question invites us to tread carefully, establishing robust ethical guidelines and regulatory frameworks that safeguard privacy while enabling innovation. It's a delicate balance, but one that is essential for the responsible use of big data.

In conclusion, big data represents a paradigm shift in how we understand and interact with the world. Its volume, velocity, variety, and veracity offer unprecedented opportunities to drive progress and innovation across every sector of society. Yet, as we unlock these opportunities, we must also confront the challenges they present, from technical hurdles to ethical dilemmas.

Big data is not just a technological trend; it's a lens through which we can view and shape the future. As we continue to demystify this complex field, let's embrace the possibilities it holds with both caution and enthusiasm. After all, in the vast ocean of data, each discovery brings us closer to understanding the world in ways we never imagined possible.

Exploring the Internet of Things (IoT)

As we navigate deeper into the digital age, the Internet of Things (IoT) emerges as a pivotal player in the symphony of big data. Imagine a world where your coffee maker knows your morning schedule, your thermostat adjusts itself based on your preferences, and streetlights in your city dim when there's no one around. This interconnected web of devices, pulsing with data, is not a snippet from a futuristic novel—it's the reality of IoT.

The IoT is a vast network of physical objects embedded with sensors, software, and other technologies for the purpose of connecting and exchanging data with other devices and systems over the Internet. These devices range from ordinary household items to sophisticated industrial tools. With over 10 billion connected IoT devices today, and this number is expected to skyrocket in the coming years, the implications for efficiency, safety, and lifestyle are profound.

Why does IoT matter in the context of big data? Each device in the IoT ecosystem acts as a data collector, contributing to the massive volume of information we described as big data. These devices collect and transmit data in real-time, adding to the velocity and variety of big data. From the perspective of veracity, IoT devices provide a wealth of accurate, sensor-generated data, enriching the quality of data available for analysis.

Let's delve into a few examples to paint a clearer picture of the IoT landscape.

Consider smart home devices, such as thermostats that learn your temperature preferences and adjust the heating or cooling to make your home more comfortable. Or smart refrigerators that track your food inventory and suggest recipes based on what you have on hand. These devices not only make daily life more convenient but also collect data on usage patterns, energy consumption, and even food preferences. This data can lead to energy savings, reduced waste, and a better understanding of consumer behavior.

Wearable health monitors represent another fascinating application of IoT. Devices like fitness trackers, smartwatches, and heart rate monitors collect data on physical activity, sleep patterns, and vital signs. This continuous stream of health-related data offers unprecedented opportunities for personalized healthcare. Doctors can monitor patients remotely, receive alerts about potential health issues before they become serious, and tailor treatments based on real-time data. The implications for preventive medicine and chronic disease management are staggering.

On a larger scale, connected urban infrastructure is transforming cities into smart cities. Sensors embedded in roads, bridges, and buildings collect data on traffic patterns, structural health, and environmental conditions. This data can improve public safety, streamline traffic flow, and guide maintenance and development efforts. Imagine a city that anticipates and mitigates traffic jams, or a bridge that alerts engineers about potential structural issues before they become hazardous.

But with great power comes great responsibility. The proliferation of IoT devices raises significant privacy and security concerns. Each connected device represents a potential entry point for cyberattacks, and the personal data collected by these devices is a treasure trove for hackers. Moreover, the question of who owns the data collected by IoT devices and how it's used is a matter of ongoing debate.

So, how do we harness the benefits of IoT while addressing these challenges?

First and foremost, robust security measures are essential. Manufacturers must prioritize security in the design of IoT devices, and users must be diligent about updating software and managing access controls. Privacy protections, including transparent data policies and user control over data collection and sharing, are also crucial.

The potential of IoT, in conjunction with big data, to revolutionize our lives is immense. From making our daily routines more convenient to enabling smarter cities and more responsive healthcare, the possibilities are limited only by our imagination—and our commitment to navigating the ethical and security challenges that accompany this technological advancement.

In this interconnected world, every device has a story to tell. As we weave these stories together, the tapestry of big data becomes richer, more complex, and infinitely more valuable. The journey through the world of IoT is just beginning, but its impact on our understanding and interaction with the world around us is already undeniable.

The IoT is not just about smart devices; it's about a smarter approach to life. With careful stewardship and a focus on the greater good, the convergence of IoT and big data can lead us into a future where technology serves humanity in ways we are only beginning to understand.

Let's embrace this journey with open minds and vigilant hearts, for the data we gather today will shape the world of tomorrow.

Big Data Analytics and IoT Synergy

As we delve further into the exploration of big data analytics and the Internet of Things (IoT), a compelling synergy emerges—one that holds the potential to reshape industries, revolutionize our daily lives, and unlock insights that were once beyond our grasp. This fusion between the massive streams of data generated by IoT devices and the sophisticated analytics that dissect this information paves the way for a future where data-driven decisions are not just an advantage but a necessity.

Imagine a world where every piece of data, no matter how minute, contributes to a larger narrative. A narrative that, when correctly interpreted, can predict failures before they occur, personalize experiences to an individual's unique needs, and optimize systems for peak efficiency. This is not the realm of fantasy but the practical reality made possible through the convergence of big data analytics and IoT.

Consider the industrial sector, where machinery and equipment are the lifelines of production. Traditional maintenance schedules rely on calendar-based or usage-based triggers, an approach that often leads to unnecessary maintenance or, worse, unexpected failures. Now, infuse IoT into the scenario. Sensors embedded in the machinery continuously collect data on temperature, vibration, power consumption, and more. This data, when analyzed, reveals patterns and anomalies that preemptively signal the need for maintenance. Suddenly, the unpredictable becomes predictable, saving time, resources, and the potential for catastrophic failure. The question then arises: How many industries can benefit from such foresight?

The energy sector provides another vivid illustration of big data analytics and IoT in harmony. Smart grids, empowered by IoT devices, gather data on consumption patterns, supply fluctuations, and operational conditions across the grid. This data, when subjected to advanced analytics, enables utilities to balance supply and demand in real time, detect faults before they lead to outages, and integrate renewable energy sources more effectively. The result? A more resilient, efficient, and sustainable energy system. One must wonder, what if every utility could predict and prevent outages before they disrupt lives?

In the realm of healthcare, the synergy between big data analytics and IoT is perhaps most transformative. Wearable devices monitor vital signs, activity levels, and other health indicators, generating a continuous stream of data. When analyzed, this data allows for personalized healthcare plans, early detection of potential health issues, and interventions tailored to the individual's specific needs. Imagine a world where healthcare is proactive, not reactive, and treatments are as unique as the individuals receiving them. How many lives could be improved, or even saved, by such personalized attention?

Urban environments, too, stand to benefit immensely from the integration of big data analytics and IoT. Sensors deployed across a city's infrastructure collect data on traffic flow, congestion points, and public transit usage. By applying analytics to this data, cities can optimize traffic patterns in real time, reduce congestion, and improve public transit efficiency. The impact extends beyond convenience, contributing to reduced emissions and enhanced quality of urban life. The question is, how can we scale these benefits to transform urban living across the globe?

At the core of these applications is the role of artificial intelligence (AI) and machine learning in processing and interpreting the vast, complex data streams generated by IoT devices. These technologies enable the identification of patterns and trends within the data, facilitating automated decision-making and predictive insights that would be impossible for humans to derive unaided. The potential is staggering, but it also raises important questions about privacy, security, and the ethical use of data. How do we navigate these challenges to ensure that the benefits of big data analytics and IoT are realized without compromising our values?

In conclusion, the synergy between big data analytics and IoT heralds a future where data not only informs but transforms decision-making across industries and aspects of daily life. From predictive maintenance and smart grids to personalized healthcare and traffic optimization, the possibilities are as vast as the data streams themselves. Yet, as we chart this promising future, we must remain vigilant stewards of the data, ensuring that its use serves the greater good and respects the privacy and security of all.

The journey into the world of big data analytics and IoT is one of discovery, innovation, and, above all, potential. It's a journey that asks us to imagine a world made better through data, and then challenges us to create it. Let's continue this journey with open minds, critical questions, and a commitment to harnessing the power of data for a brighter, more efficient, and more personalized future.

Ethical and Privacy Implications

In the dazzling landscape that big data analytics and the Internet of Things (IoT) have unveiled, a shadow looms, one that demands our vigilant attention. This shadow is cast by the ethical considerations and privacy concerns inherent in the collection, analysis, and application of vast datasets. At the heart of this issue lies the potential for surveillance, data breaches, and the misuse of personal information, which underscores the critical need for robust data governance, security measures, and ethical guidelines.

Imagine, for a moment, a world where every online search, every step you take, and every heartbeat is not just monitored but analyzed and stored. This isn't the plot of a dystopian novel; it's a reality that's inching closer with the advancement of IoT devices and big data technologies. The convenience and personalized experience these technologies offer come with a hidden cost: our privacy.

But what does privacy really mean in a world awash with data? It's the right to have a say in what information about us is collected and how it's used. Yet, as we've seen, the boundaries of this right are constantly being tested and, often, breached. Data breaches have become all too common, exposing sensitive personal information to those with malicious intent. The repercussions of these breaches extend beyond the immediate stress and financial harm to victims; they erode trust in the very technologies that promise to enhance our lives.

Surveillance, both governmental and corporate, is another facet of this complex issue. With the capability to track and analyze our every move, the line between safeguarding the public and infringing on individual freedoms becomes blurred. How do we navigate this delicate balance? The answer lies in establishing stringent ethical guidelines and governance structures that prioritize individuals' rights and privacy.

DATA DEMYSTIFIED: A BEGINNER'S GUIDE TO UNDERSTANDING THE WORLD THROUGH NUMBERS

Data governance encompasses the policies, standards, and practices that ensure data is used ethically and responsibly. Effective governance requires transparency about what data is collected, how it's processed, and for what purposes. Furthermore, individuals must have control over their own data, including the ability to access, correct, and even erase their information.

Security measures, too, play a crucial role in protecting privacy. These measures include not only technical solutions like encryption and secure data storage but also policies that limit access to data and regular audits to ensure compliance with privacy laws and regulations.

Ethical guidelines, however, are the foundation upon which privacy and data governance rest. These guidelines should promote fairness, accountability, and respect for individuals' rights. They must address the challenges posed by new technologies, guiding developers, users, and policymakers in the responsible use of data.

Consider the implications of predictive analytics in healthcare, a field where the benefits of big data and IoT are undeniable. While predictive models can significantly improve patient outcomes, they also raise concerns about consent and the potential for discrimination. Ethical guidelines in this context might mandate informed consent for the use of personal health data and require that predictive models are transparent and free from bias.

The road ahead is fraught with challenges, but also filled with promise. As we continue to navigate the complex landscape of big data and IoT, let us do so with a commitment to protecting the privacy and dignity of individuals. Let us be the architects of a future where technology serves humanity, guided by robust data governance, stringent security measures, and unwavering ethical principles.

One cannot help but wonder, what will this future look like? Will we rise to the challenge of safeguarding our privacy while reaping the benefits of big data and IoT, or will we falter, ensnared by the very technologies we sought to master?

The choice is ours to make. Let's choose wisely.

The Future of Big Data and IoT

As we stand on the brink of a new era, the future of big data and the Internet of Things (IoT) beckons with a blend of promise and uncertainty. Emerging technologies are rapidly reshaping the landscape, offering unprecedented opportunities to understand and interact with the world around us. Yet, as we venture further into this uncharted territory, the balance between technological innovation and ethical considerations becomes increasingly delicate.

Imagine a city where traffic flows smoothly, guided by a network of sensors and smart algorithms that predict and manage congestion in real time. Picture a healthcare system where wearable devices and remote monitoring tools empower individuals to manage their health proactively, with personalized insights derived from vast datasets. These scenarios are not mere fantasies but glimpses of a future made possible by the synergy of big data and IoT.

The advent of next-generation networks, like 5G, is set to turbocharge this evolution. With its promise of lightning-fast speeds, near-zero latency, and the capacity to connect a staggering number of devices, 5G is poised to unlock the full potential of IoT solutions. The implications for data volume and analysis capabilities are profound. As the fabric of connectivity grows denser, the flow of data becomes a torrent, offering deeper insights but also raising critical questions about how we manage, protect, and leverage this wealth of information.

How do we navigate this future without losing sight of our values and ethical principles? The answer lies in embracing a framework that prioritizes human dignity, privacy, and the common good. As we marvel at the possibilities, we must also confront the challenges head-on, engaging in a thoughtful dialogue about the societal impacts of these technologies.

Consider the delicate balance between convenience and surveillance. The same technologies that simplify our lives also have the potential to erode our privacy, turning every interaction and movement into data points to be analyzed and monetized. Here, the role of policy and regulation becomes paramount. We must advocate for frameworks that not only foster innovation but also protect individual rights and promote transparency and accountability.

Ethical considerations extend beyond privacy. As algorithms play an increasingly central role in decision-making, from credit scoring to job recruitment, the risk of bias and discrimination looms large. Ensuring that these algorithms are fair, transparent, and accountable is not just a technical challenge but a moral imperative. The quest for efficiency must not override the principles of equity and justice.

In this future, the role of education cannot be overstated. Empowering individuals with the knowledge and skills to navigate the digital landscape is crucial. Literacy in data and technology becomes as fundamental as reading and writing, enabling people to critically engage with the tools and platforms that shape their lives.

One-line paragraphs can be powerful. They can make us stop and think.

As we look to the future, let's envision a world where big data and IoT serve as instruments of empowerment, not tools of control. A world where technology enhances our humanity, bridging divides and fostering a more inclusive and equitable society. This vision is not beyond our reach, but realizing it requires a collective effort. It demands that we, as a global community, commit to guiding the development of these technologies with a keen eye on their societal impacts, grounded in a framework of ethical principles.

The future of big data and IoT is undeniably exciting, filled with possibilities that stretch the limits of our imagination. Yet, as we stand at this crossroads, we must choose the path forward carefully. The choices we make today will shape the world for generations to come.

So, what will it be?

With every step into this brave new world, let's carry with us a sense of responsibility, a commitment to ethical stewardship, and a vision of a future where technology and humanity walk hand in hand. A future where big data and IoT continue to transform lives, not by diminishing our privacy and values, but by enriching them, ensuring a legacy that future generations will thank us for.

The journey ahead is ours to chart. Together, let's embrace the promise of big data and IoT, navigating this complex landscape with wisdom, courage, and an unwavering commitment to the greater good.

Artificial Intelligence and Machine Learning

Demystifying AI and Machine Learning

In the luminous dawn of the digital age, a groundbreaking revolution began to unfurl, weaving the intricate tapestry of Artificial Intelligence (AI) and Machine Learning (ML). As we embark on this journey to demystify these concepts, let's first dismantle the fortress of confusion surrounding them. What exactly is AI? And how does ML fit into this futuristic puzzle?

Imagine, if you will, a world where machines can think, learn, and make decisions akin to a human. This is the realm of Artificial Intelligence. At its core, AI is the creation of intelligent machines that can perform tasks requiring human intelligence. These tasks include understanding natural language, recognizing patterns and images, making decisions, and even playing complex games. It's like teaching a child to solve puzzles; the child learns, adapts, and eventually masters the task.

Nestled within the expansive domain of AI, Machine Learning stands as a shining beacon, a subset focused on algorithms that learn from data. Think of ML as teaching a computer to learn from past experiences. If AI is the goal of creating intelligence, ML is the path that leads there, allowing machines to improve at their tasks with experience, much like a student becoming more skilled with study.

But how does ML work, exactly? Imagine feeding a computer thousands of pictures of cats and dogs. Over time, the computer begins to notice the differences between them on its own. It learns, for instance, that cats often have sharper ears and dogs have longer noses. This is ML in action: learning from data to make predictions or decisions.

Now, let's address a common misconception: the idea that AI and ML are distant, futuristic concepts. In reality, they are here, seamlessly integrated into our daily lives. When Netflix recommends a movie you might like, that's ML analyzing your viewing history. When you ask Siri or Alexa a question and receive an answer, that's AI in motion, understanding and processing your language.

But, why does this matter to you? Imagine the possibilities if we could predict natural disasters with greater accuracy, personalize education to each student's learning style, or diagnose diseases earlier than ever before. AI and ML are not just about robots and science fiction; they're about enhancing human capabilities and making the impossible possible.

Diving deeper, consider the implications of AI and ML in the realm of data analysis. Data, in its raw form, can be overwhelming and cryptic. However, through the lens of ML, this data transforms into insights and knowledge. It's akin to finding patterns in the stars; what once seemed random now reveals constellations.

Yet, with great power comes great responsibility. As we harness AI and ML, ethical considerations must be at the forefront. We must ask ourselves: How do we ensure fairness in AI decisions? How do we protect privacy when machines can learn so much about us?

This chapter is only the beginning, a mere scratching of the surface of the vast and complex world of AI and ML. Throughout, we've used analogies to bridge the gap between these high-tech concepts and everyday experiences, making the complex accessible and the abstract tangible.

In this exploration, we've seen how AI aims to replicate human intelligence in machines, while ML provides these machines with the ability to learn and improve from experience. We've debunked myths, brought to light the everyday applications of these technologies, and pondered their implications for the future.

As we stand on the brink of this new era, one question remains: How will we navigate the future of AI and ML? The answer lies not in the stars, but in our hands, as we guide these technologies towards a future that enhances, rather than diminishes, the human experience.

Let us move forward with curiosity, caution, and an unwavering commitment to using AI and ML as tools for positive change. In doing so, we not only demystify these concepts but also unlock their potential to reshape our world.

Remember, the journey through the world of data and numbers is not about reaching a destination. It's about understanding the path, the patterns, and the possibilities that lie ahead. And so, as we close this chapter, let us embrace the journey of demystifying AI and ML, armed with knowledge, and inspired by the endless potential to innovate and improve the world around us.

The Intersection of Data With AI/ML

As we venture deeper into the labyrinth of modern technology, a profound intersection emerges, one where the realms of Artificial Intelligence (AI) and Machine Learning (ML) converge with the vast universe of data. This juncture, brimming with opportunities and challenges, holds the key to unlocking a future where machines not only mimic human intelligence but also evolve through learning. This chapter aims to demystify this critical intersection, illuminating the path for those embarking on the quest to understand the world through numbers.

At the heart of AI and ML lies an insatiable hunger for data. Data, in its essence, serves as the nourishment that fuels the sophisticated algorithms driving AI and ML. Without it, these technologies would remain dormant, unable to unleash their true potential. But why does data hold such power? And how does its quality, diversity, and structure influence the effectiveness of AI and ML models?

Imagine teaching a child to recognize fruits by showing them pictures. If you only show them apples, they might struggle to identify a banana when they see one. Similarly, AI and ML models thrive on diverse and high-quality data, enabling them to learn, adapt, and perform a wide array of tasks with remarkable accuracy. The richness of data ensures that models are well-rounded, capable of understanding the nuances of the world they are designed to interpret.

Structured, unstructured, and semi-structured data form the triad that AI and ML algorithms navigate. Structured data, organized and easily searchable, includes databases of numbers and text. Unstructured data, chaotic and messy, encompasses emails, videos, and social media posts. Semi-structured data, a blend of the two, might include emails coded with tags that make certain elements searchable. Each type presents unique challenges and opportunities for AI and ML, from parsing through the syntax of human language in unstructured data to extracting insights from the rigid confines of structured datasets.

Now, let the curtains rise on the practical applications of AI and ML, where these technologies leap from theory to the tangible world. Picture the recommendation systems on streaming platforms like Netflix or Spotify. By analyzing your viewing or listening history, these systems predict what you might enjoy next, creating a personalized entertainment experience. This marvel of technology relies on vast amounts of data and sophisticated ML algorithms to understand your preferences better than you might yourself.

Consider the predictive text feature in messaging apps. As you type, the app suggests the next word, learning from your writing style and commonly used phrases. This convenience, now taken for granted, stems from ML models trained on massive datasets of text, learning the intricacies of language and human communication.

In the realm of healthcare, diagnostic tools powered by AI and ML are revolutionizing the way diseases are detected and treated. By analyzing medical images, these tools can identify patterns invisible to the human eye, aiding in early diagnosis and potentially saving lives. Again, the underlying force is data – diverse, high-quality, and meticulously annotated datasets that teach the models to distinguish between health and disease.

As we navigate this intersection of data with AI and ML, several questions beckon our attention. How do we ensure the ethical use of data, respecting privacy and consent? What measures can we take to mitigate biases in AI and ML models, ensuring fairness and inclusivity? The road ahead calls for a balanced approach, one that harnesses the power of data and technology to improve lives while upholding ethical standards and human values.

In this chapter, we have journeyed through the landscape where data meets AI and ML, uncovering the intricacies and marvels along the path. This exploration serves not just to enlighten but also to inspire, urging us to envision a future where technology and humanity converge in harmony. As we stand at this crossroads, the choices we make will shape the trajectory of AI and ML, steering these technologies towards a future that reflects our highest aspirations.

The intersection of data with AI and ML is not just a technical waypoint; it's a beacon of potential, illuminating the possibilities that lie ahead. As we continue our quest to understand the world through numbers, let us embrace this intersection with curiosity, responsibility, and a steadfast commitment to leveraging technology for the betterment of humanity.

Transformative Potential of AI and ML

In the previous exploration of the intersection between data, Artificial Intelligence (AI), and Machine Learning (ML), we ventured into the realms where technology and humanity converge. As we proceed, it becomes imperative to delve deeper into the transformative potential of AI and ML, unraveling how these technologies are not merely tools but catalysts for unprecedented change.

Embarking on this journey, one cannot help but wonder, what is it about AI and ML that sets them apart as harbingers of transformation? The answer lies in their unique ability to learn from data, to adapt, and to make decisions with minimal human intervention. This capability, though profoundly technical, harbors the power to reshape industries, redefine our daily lives, and even alter the fabric of society.

Consider the agricultural sector, a realm traditionally governed by the cycles of nature and human labor. Today, AI-driven technologies are revolutionizing farming practices, enabling precision agriculture. Sensors deployed across fields collect data on soil moisture, temperature, and nutrient levels. AI algorithms analyze this data, offering insights that help farmers optimize irrigation, fertilization, and harvesting schedules. The result? Higher yields, reduced waste, and a smaller environmental footprint. Through these changes, AI and ML breathe new life into an age-old industry, demonstrating that even the most traditional sectors can be reimagined.

In the bustling streets of urban landscapes, AI and ML are weaving their magic in the realm of transportation. Autonomous vehicles, once a figment of science fiction, are becoming a reality, promising to transform our commuting experiences. Powered by AI algorithms that process data from sensors and cameras, these vehicles navigate roads with precision, reducing the likelihood of accidents caused by human error. The vision of a future where traffic flows smoothly, and roads are safer, is inching closer to reality, thanks to the advancements in AI and ML.

But the transformative potential of AI and ML extends beyond economic and practical applications. These technologies also hold the promise of enhancing our understanding of the human condition itself. In the field of mental health, for example, AI-powered tools are offering new insights into the complexities of the human mind. By analyzing patterns in speech and writing, AI can help identify early signs of conditions such as depression or anxiety, often before individuals themselves are aware. This opens the door to early intervention and a personalized approach to mental health care, highlighting the profound impact AI and ML can have on our well-being.

Yet, as we stand on the cusp of these transformative changes, questions loom large. How do we navigate the ethical dilemmas posed by AI and ML? Can we ensure that the benefits of these technologies are equitably distributed, avoiding the pitfalls of exacerbating inequalities?

To address these challenges, a collaborative approach is essential. Policymakers, technologists, and society at large must engage in open dialogue, crafting frameworks that prioritize ethical considerations and inclusivity. Only by working together can we harness the full potential of AI and ML, steering these technologies towards outcomes that reflect our shared values and aspirations.

As we contemplate the road ahead, it becomes clear that the journey with AI and ML is not just about technological innovation. It's about reimagining what's possible, about daring to dream of a future where technology amplifies our human potential. This journey is ours to embark upon, armed with curiosity, guided by ethics, and driven by a commitment to creating a world where technology serves humanity's highest ideals.

In the grand narrative of human progress, AI and ML are not mere chapters. They are the unfolding stories of transformation, a testament to our relentless pursuit of knowledge and our undying hope for a better tomorrow. As we venture forward, let us embrace the transformative potential of AI and ML, not just as tools for change, but as companions in our quest to understand the world through numbers, and, more importantly, through the lens of our shared humanity.

The transformative potential of AI and ML awaits. Are we ready to journey into this new horizon, to shape and be shaped by the technologies of tomorrow? The answer lies within us, in our capacity to dream, to innovate, and to create a future that mirrors our collective aspirations.

With every step we take into the unknown, let us remember: the future is not something we enter. The future is something we create, together, through the transformative power of AI and ML.

Ethical Considerations and Societal Impacts

In the sprawling landscape of technological evolution, the ethical considerations and societal impacts of Artificial Intelligence (AI) and Machine Learning (ML) stand as towering signposts, guiding us through a terrain fraught with complexity and moral ambiguity. These technologies, while promising to catapult humanity into an era of unprecedented efficiency and innovation, also beckon us to tread carefully, to ponder the weight of our creations on the scales of ethics and social justice.

Imagine a world where decision-making systems, devoid of human prejudice, administer justice with absolute fairness. Yet, paradoxically, the algorithms that power these systems are not born in a vacuum. They are shaped by human hands and, consequently, can inherit our biases. Instances abound where AI systems have exhibited racial, gender, or socioeconomic biases, inadvertently amplifying societal inequalities. The question then arises, how do we cleanse the lens through which AI views our world?

Transparency in AI development becomes a beacon of hope in this regard. By shedding light on the inner workings of algorithms, we foster a climate of trust and understanding. However, the path to achieving true transparency is strewn with technical and ethical challenges. The intricate complexity of ML models often makes them inscrutable, even to their creators. This opacity, termed the "black box" phenomenon, poses a significant hurdle to accountability. Can trust truly flourish in the shadow of the unknown?

In addressing these conundrums, the involvement of diverse teams in AI/ML projects emerges as a critical piece of the puzzle. Diversity, in this context, transcends gender, race, and cultural backgrounds, encompassing a broad spectrum of experiences, perspectives, and cognitive approaches. A mosaic of voices, each contributing their unique insight, can illuminate blind spots, ensuring that AI systems are designed with inclusivity and fairness at their core.

Yet, the journey does not end here. The development of guidelines and standards for ethical AI use is a collective endeavor, requiring the harmonious collaboration of governments, corporations, academia, and civil society. This collaborative effort aims to weave a tapestry of principles that balance innovation with social responsibility, guiding the AI odyssey towards a future where technology uplifts humanity.

The societal impacts of AI and ML extend their tendrils into the very fabric of our existence, reshaping the landscape of employment, privacy, and democracy. As machines become capable of performing tasks once thought uniquely human, the specter of job displacement looms large. However, this challenge also harbors the seed of opportunity—the chance to redefine work, to imbue it with greater creativity and meaning. How do we seize this moment to sculpt a future where technology amplifies human potential rather than diminishing it?

DATA DEMYSTIFIED: A BEGINNER'S GUIDE TO UNDERSTANDING THE WORLD THROUGH NUMBERS

Privacy, the sanctum of our individuality, faces its own set of trials in the age of AI. In a world awash with data, the boundaries between public and private blur, raising profound questions about surveillance, consent, and the right to be forgotten. As AI systems weave ever more intricate tapestries of our personal lives, the need for robust privacy protections becomes paramount. Can we navigate this delicate balance, ensuring that AI serves as a tool for empowerment rather than a mechanism of control?

Moreover, the influence of AI on public opinion and democracy cannot be overstated. In an era where algorithms curate the reality we encounter online, the potential for manipulation looms as a dark cloud over the digital horizon. The integrity of our democratic processes hinges on our ability to foster an information ecosystem that values truth, diversity of thought, and open dialogue. The question before us is stark: will AI be a force that fragments our societal fabric, or will it serve to strengthen the bonds of our collective humanity?

As we stand at this crossroads, gazing into the future with a mixture of hope and trepidation, the responsibility that accompanies the power of AI and ML becomes ever more apparent. We are the architects of this new world, and with each line of code, with every algorithm we design, we cast a stone into the foundation of tomorrow.

The ethical considerations and societal impacts of AI and ML are not mere academic musings; they are the very essence of our journey into the digital age. In this quest, our compass is not technology itself, but the values we hold dear—fairness, transparency, inclusivity, and accountability. As we navigate the turbulent waters of innovation, let us anchor ourselves to these principles, for they are the stars by which we can chart a course to a future where technology amplifies the best of what it means to be human.

In the grand tapestry of human endeavor, AI and ML represent threads of immense potential. Woven with care, they can create a future vibrant with possibility, a testament to our highest aspirations. The path is ours to choose, and the time to act is now.

Navigating the Future With AI and ML

Navigating the future with Artificial Intelligence (AI) and Machine Learning (ML) requires not just an understanding of these technologies but an embrace of the changes they herald. As we stand on the brink of a new era, where digital literacy becomes as fundamental as reading and writing, the question isn't if we will adapt, but how swiftly and effectively we can do so. The world is transforming, and with it, the very fabric of our daily lives. The horizon is bright, albeit peppered with challenges that demand our attention and ingenuity.

The advent of generative AI is a beacon, signaling a future where machines can create, innovate, and maybe even 'think' in ways previously reserved for humans. This technology, capable of producing original content—from art to literature, and even code—promises to revolutionize industries. Yet, with its rise, we must ponder: How will human creativity be valued? The allure of this question lies not in fear but in the potential for collaboration between human and machine, a synergy that could elevate our creative endeavors to unprecedented heights.

Simultaneously, advancements in natural language processing (NLP) are demolishing the barriers of communication. Imagine a world where language is no longer a barrier but a bridge, connecting minds and hearts across the globe. This reality is within our grasp. However, as machines grow more adept at understanding and generating human language, we must remain vigilant. The nuances of culture, emotion, and intention are delicate; preserving these in a world mediated by technology is paramount.

The potential for AI to tackle complex global challenges is perhaps the most inspiring. Climate change, poverty, disease—these titans of our time may finally meet their match. AI's capacity to analyze vast datasets and model complex systems offers a beacon of hope. But with great power comes great responsibility. The decisions we make, the algorithms we design, and the data we use to feed them—each of these elements holds the potential to shape our world for better or worse.

DATA DEMYSTIFIED: A BEGINNER'S GUIDE TO UNDERSTANDING THE WORLD THROUGH NUMBERS

So, how do we navigate this future?

Lifelong learning emerges as a non-negotiable. The notion that education ends upon leaving the classroom is obsolete. The future belongs to those willing to continuously evolve, to learn and unlearn in the face of relentless change. Digital literacy is no longer optional. Understanding the basics of AI and ML, the ethical implications, and the societal impacts of these technologies is crucial. This knowledge empowers us to make informed decisions, to engage in meaningful conversations about the direction we wish our world to take.

Preparation for a world shaped by AI and ML also involves fostering flexibility and resilience. The job landscape is transforming, with automation replacing certain roles and creating others. Embracing this change, redefining our relationship with work, and finding value in human skills that machines cannot replicate—creativity, empathy, critical thinking—will be key.

Amidst these changes, ethical considerations remain at the forefront. As we speculate on the future, envisioning a world enriched by AI and ML, we must also anchor ourselves to the values that define our humanity. Transparency, fairness, inclusivity—these principles must guide the development and deployment of technology.

Emerging trends in AI and ML, such as generative AI and advanced NLP, bring us to the cusp of a new world. A world where machines can create, communicate, and perhaps even understand in ways that mimic human intelligence. The potential for AI to address monumental challenges and enrich our lives is immense. Yet, as we chart this course, we must remain vigilant stewards of the technology we create.

The journey ahead is as daunting as it is exhilarating. But remember, the stars that once guided ancient mariners across vast, unknown oceans were not there to dictate their path but to offer a bearing. In the same way, the emerging trends in AI and ML are not blueprints but beacons—points of light illuminating the vast potential of what we can achieve together.

Let us step into this future with open minds and hearts, ready to learn, adapt, and grow. Let us not shy away from the challenges but meet them with courage and creativity. For in our hands lies not just the power to shape the future of technology but to ensure that it reflects the best of what it means to be human.

Protecting Your Data

Understanding Data Privacy and Security

In this interconnected world, the significance of data privacy and security can hardly be overstated. Imagine, if you will, a place where every whisper, every transaction, and every fleeting thought is not only recorded but laid bare for the world to see. This, unfortunately, is not as much a dystopian fantasy as one might hope, but rather a reflection of our current reality, where personal and sensitive information is stored and processed online, often with scant regard for the implications.

Data privacy, fundamentally, is the right to have control over how your personal information is collected and used. It's the concept that allows you to walk the digital streets without the fear of your every move being tracked and cataloged. Security, on the other hand, is the gallant guardian that protects data from unauthorized access and corruption throughout its lifecycle. Together, they form the bulwark that shields our digital selves.

Consider the act of online shopping, a routine as mundane as it is necessary in our modern lives. With each click, personal information—names, addresses, credit card numbers—travels through the ether, passing from your fingertips to the store's database. Herein lies vulnerability. Without robust security measures, this data could easily fall into the wrong hands, leading to identity theft, financial loss, and a profound sense of violation.

Or take social media, a realm where people share not just thoughts, but intimate moments of their lives. Without strict privacy controls and an understanding of what is shared publicly, personal information can become fodder for advertisers, or worse, malicious actors.

Why should this matter to you? Imagine receiving a letter that was meant to be private, only to find it opened and read by someone else. That intrusion, that breach of trust, is what happens on a grand scale when data privacy and security are not taken seriously.

In the realm of data, encryption acts as a powerful ally. It scrambles information so that it can only be deciphered by someone with the correct key. Think of it as sending a message in a bottle with a lock only the intended recipient can open.

But it's not just about technology. Legislation plays a crucial role too. Laws like the General Data Protection Regulation (GDPR) in the European Union empower individuals by granting them rights over their data. They can decide who gets to see it, how it's used, and even demand it be deleted.

Still, the question lingers in the air: How can one navigate this digital landscape safely?

First and foremost, awareness is the lantern that lights the path. Knowing what information you're sharing and with whom is the cornerstone of data privacy. Simple actions, like reading the privacy policies of websites and apps, while admittedly tedious, are essential steps in protecting oneself.

Moreover, utilizing strong, unique passwords and employing two-factor authentication wherever possible fortify the walls around your digital presence. Think of each password as a key, and the more complex it is, the harder it is for someone else to replicate.

But let's not forget, the responsibility doesn't lie with individuals alone. Companies must hold themselves to the highest standards of data protection, treating the information entrusted to them with the utmost care and respect.

A breach of data security is not just an inconvenience. It's a violation that can have ripple effects, touching every aspect of a person's life. Stories abound of individuals who, through no fault of their own, have found themselves ensnared in a nightmare of identity theft and financial fraud.

In conclusion, the digital world offers boundless opportunities, but it also presents new risks. Data privacy and security are the shields that protect our personal information from being exploited. As we navigate this digital age, let us do so with caution and respect for the power of the data we hold in our hands.

Remember, in the vast expanse of the internet, a little knowledge and a lot of caution can make all the difference. Let us be vigilant. Let us be safe. And above all, let us understand the value of the information that defines our digital selves.

Risks and Threats to Personal Data

In the labyrinthine expanse of the digital world, myriad risks and threats loom, ever ready to exploit the smallest of openings in our defenses. These threats are not merely nuisances; they are formidable adversaries that can wreak havoc on an individual's life, leading to consequences as dire as identity theft, financial ruin, and irrevocable privacy invasions. So, what makes our personal data so vulnerable, and what are these shadowy forces that seek to exploit it?

Cyberattacks, a term that conjures images of shadowy figures typing in dimly lit rooms, are indeed a significant threat to our personal data. These attacks are multifaceted, targeting the infrastructure of the internet, corporate databases, and unsuspecting individuals alike. A particularly insidious form is the Distributed Denial of Service (DDoS) attack, which can overwhelm systems, rendering them inoperative and leaving data exposed. Imagine a fortress under siege, its gates battered by an unrelenting force until, inevitably, they give way.

Phishing scams, on the other hand, rely not on brute force but on deception. They are the digital equivalent of a Trojan horse, tricking the unsuspecting into handing over their data willingly. An email that appears to be from a trusted source, asking you to verify your account details, might seem innocuous. But in reality, it's a deceit, a facade designed to lure you into a trap. Once the information is given, the damage is done.

Malware, a portmanteau of 'malicious software,' is another formidable opponent. This term encompasses viruses, worms, ransomware, and spyware, each designed to infiltrate, damage, or take control of a computer system without the user's consent. Ransomware, for instance, locks users out of their systems, holding their data hostage until a ransom is paid. It's akin to coming home to find a lock on your door that only the burglar has the key to.

Data breaches, unfortunately, have become all too common. These occur when confidential information is accessed without authorization, often due to inadequate security measures. The consequences can be devastating, with sensitive data, from social security numbers to bank account details, falling into the wrong hands. It's like a vault, thought to be secure, suddenly cracked open for all to see.

But why are these threats so successful? They prey on the two most vulnerable aspects of the digital ecosystem: system flaws and human error. Systems, no matter how robust, can have weaknesses, and attackers are adept at finding and exploiting these chinks in the armor. Human error, however, is perhaps even more significant. A moment of inattention, a lapse in judgment, or a lack of knowledge can open the door to attackers.

The consequences of these vulnerabilities being exploited can range from the inconvenient to the catastrophic. At the less severe end of the spectrum, individuals might experience annoying spam emails or minor disruptions to their digital services. Far more concerning, however, are the instances of identity theft, where criminals assume an individual's identity to commit fraud. This can lead to financial losses, damage to credit scores, and a long, arduous process of reclaiming one's identity.

Moreover, the emotional toll should not be underestimated. Victims of cyberattacks often report feeling violated, as if their personal space has been intruded upon. This psychological impact, coupled with the potential for public embarrassment and the strain of financial recovery, can be overwhelming.

So, what can be done to mitigate these risks? The first step is awareness. Understanding the nature of these threats is akin to recognizing the face of your enemy. Vigilance is also crucial. Regularly updating software, using strong, unique passwords, and being skeptical of unsolicited requests for information are all basic but effective defenses.

Remember, the digital world is not a passive environment; it is a dynamic battlefield where the threats evolve as rapidly as the technologies designed to thwart them. As individuals, our best defense is a combination of knowledge, caution, and a proactive approach to our digital hygiene.

At this juncture, one might wonder, is all hope lost? Absolutely not. The key lies in empowerment through education. By demystifying data and understanding the risks, individuals can take control, safeguarding their digital presence against the myriad threats that lurk in the shadows.

In conclusion, the risks and threats to personal data are numerous and varied, ranging from cyberattacks to phishing scams, malware, and data breaches. These threats exploit system vulnerabilities and human behavior to access or steal data, leading to potential consequences such as identity theft, financial loss, and privacy invasions. However, by being aware, vigilant, and proactive, individuals can protect themselves and navigate the digital world with confidence. Remember, knowledge is power, and in the battle for data security, it is our most potent weapon.

Best Practices for Data Protection

In the ever-evolving landscape of the digital age, protecting one's data is not just advisable; it is imperative. As we navigate through the vast ocean of information available at our fingertips, the responsibility of safeguarding our personal data falls squarely on our shoulders. But where does one begin? The answer lies in adopting a series of best practices designed to fortify our digital defenses against the relentless onslaught of cyber threats.

Creating strong, unique passwords is the first line of defense in the arsenal of data protection strategies. A robust password acts as a formidable barrier, deterring unauthorized access to your digital accounts. Imagine your password as the key to a treasure chest; the more intricate the key, the less likely a pirate is to replicate it. Employ the use of password managers to generate and store complex passwords, ensuring that each of your digital accounts is secured with a unique key, thereby minimizing the risk of a domino effect should one account be compromised.

The advent of two-factor authentication (2FA) has added an additional layer of security, akin to a moat around a castle. Even if the castle key (your password) falls into the wrong hands, the moat (2FA) serves as a deterrent, preventing adversaries from breaching the castle walls. This security measure requires not only something you know (your password) but also something you have (a mobile device, for instance) to gain access. Enabling 2FA on all your accounts significantly reduces the likelihood of unauthorized access, serving as a critical checkpoint in the defense of your personal data.

But what of the cunning tricks employed by cybercriminals to lure individuals into willingly handing over their information? Phishing attempts, those deceptive emails or messages that masquerade as legitimate communications, prey on the unsuspecting. Recognizing these attempts is akin to discerning a wolf in sheep's clothing. Be wary of unsolicited requests for personal information or urgent calls to action that seem out of place. Always verify the authenticity of the communication by contacting the supposed sender through official channels. Remember, vigilance and skepticism are your allies in identifying and thwarting phishing attempts.

The sanctity of your home network, often overlooked, is a cornerstone in the edifice of digital security. Securing this network requires a multifaceted approach. Begin by changing the default name and password of your router, thus cloaking your digital abode in a veil of anonymity. Employ the use of strong encryption settings, such as WPA3, to create a robust barrier against intruders. Regularly updating the router's firmware closes any backdoors that might have been left ajar, ensuring your home network remains an impenetrable fortress.

In this age of constant connectivity, the importance of regular software updates cannot be overstated. Each update serves as a patch, mending the vulnerabilities in the fabric of your digital environment. Neglecting these updates is akin to leaving your front door unlocked, inviting nefarious elements to waltz in unchallenged. Set your devices to update automatically, ensuring you're always fortified with the latest defenses against cyber threats.

DATA DEMYSTIFIED: A BEGINNER'S GUIDE TO UNDERSTANDING THE WORLD THROUGH NUMBERS

The realm of the internet is a public square, bustling with activity. In such an environment, cautious sharing of personal information is paramount. Before divulging any piece of information, ask yourself, "Is this necessary?" Oversharing online is akin to leaving personal documents scattered in the town square, vulnerable to prying eyes. Limit the personal details you share on social media and other platforms, safeguarding your privacy against those who may exploit it.

In the quest for enhanced privacy, tools such as Virtual Private Networks (VPNs) and encrypted messaging services are invaluable allies. A VPN cloaks your online presence, shielding your activities from the gaze of unwanted observers. It's akin to moving through the digital realm under the cover of an invisibility cloak. Similarly, encrypted messaging services ensure that your communications remain confidential, visible only to you and the intended recipient. In a world where digital eavesdropping is all too common, these tools offer a haven of privacy.

To navigate the digital world safely and confidently, one must arm oneself with knowledge and the right tools. Adopting these best practices for data protection is not merely a recommendation; it is a necessity in the age of information. By fortifying your digital defenses, you ensure that your personal data remains just that—personal. Let us not forget, in the vast expanse of the digital age, vigilance is the watchword, and education is the beacon that guides us through the darkness.

In conclusion, the journey through the digital landscape is fraught with perils, but also filled with potential. By adhering to these best practices for data protection, we not only safeguard our personal information but also empower ourselves to explore the digital world with confidence. Remember, the power to protect your data is in your hands; wield it wisely.

Legal Frameworks and Rights

In the labyrinth of the digital age, laws and regulations serve as the guiding lights that ensure our personal data does not fall prey to the shadows. With the advent of regulations such as the General Data Protection Regulation (GDPR) in the European Union and the California Consumer Privacy Act (CCPA), a new era of data privacy and security awareness has dawned. These legal frameworks are not just a set of rules; they are a testament to the evolving relationship between technology and personal freedom.

At the heart of the GDPR, implemented on May 25, 2018, lies the principle of giving control back to EU residents over their personal data. Imagine walking through a market where every stall knows your name, preferences, and even your daily routines. Unsettling, isn't it? The GDPR aims to drape a cloak of anonymity over you, ensuring that your data is not misused. It mandates that organizations must seek explicit consent before collecting or processing personal data, making the act of sharing data a choice, not a compulsion.

But the GDPR goes beyond mere consent. Have you ever wondered what happens to your data after you share it? The regulation empowers individuals with the right to access their data, to see exactly what information organizations hold about them. It's akin to having a map that shows where pieces of your digital self are scattered. Moreover, if you find any of this information to be incorrect or no longer relevant, you have the right to have it corrected or deleted. This is not just about correcting errors; it's about reclaiming your narrative in the digital world.

Crossing the Atlantic, the CCPA shines as a beacon of data privacy rights in the United States. Effective from January 1, 2020, it mirrors the GDPR's ethos but tailors it to the Californian context. Under the CCPA, residents of California can not only request to see their personal data but also find out whether their data is being sold and to whom. Picture yourself as the owner of a diary filled with personal secrets. The CCPA ensures that you know who is reading your diary and gives you the power to close it anytime you wish.

One of the most compelling aspects of the CCPA is the right to non-discrimination. This means that choosing to protect your data should not come at a penalty. Imagine opting out of data sharing, only to find services and prices suddenly become less favorable. The CCPA safeguards against such scenarios, ensuring that privacy is a right, not a luxury.

DATA DEMYSTIFIED: A BEGINNER'S GUIDE TO UNDERSTANDING THE WORLD THROUGH NUMBERS

At this juncture, a question arises: How do these laws affect organizations? The onus of protecting data, under these regulations, falls heavily on the shoulders of companies and institutions. They are required to implement stringent data protection measures and to report any breaches within a set timeframe. Picture a castle guarding treasures; these treasures are your personal data. The castle walls must be robust, the guards vigilant, and any breach must sound the alarm bells not just within the castle, but across the land.

Organizations are now architects of trust. They must not only protect the data but also ensure transparency about how they use it. Failure to comply with these regulations can result in hefty fines, but perhaps more significantly, a loss of public trust. It's a reminder that in the digital bazaar, trust is the currency of value.

Let's pause for a moment. Have you ever felt a sense of unease about how your data is used? These regulations are a response to that unease, an attempt to shift the balance of power back to the individual. They are a recognition that in a world where data is gold, the rights of the individual are paramount.

In conclusion, the GDPR and CCPA are not just acronyms or a set of legal requirements. They are milestones in the journey towards a more secure and private digital future. A future where our digital selves are protected, where organizations act as guardians of our data, and where privacy is woven into the fabric of the digital age. The path is long, and the challenges many, but with these legal frameworks as our guide, the direction is clear.

As we navigate this complex landscape, remember, knowledge is your compass. Understanding your rights and the obligations of organizations is the first step towards safeguarding your digital future. Let's walk this path together, with eyes wide open and a determination to reclaim our privacy. In the vast expanse of the internet, let's make our mark, not as data points, but as individuals whose rights are inviolable.

The journey continues.

The Future of Data Privacy and Security

In the sprawling digital ecosystem where data flows like rivers through the landscape of our daily lives, the future of data privacy and security emerges as a horizon filled with both promise and peril. As we stand at this precipice, looking into the vast unknown, it's imperative to ponder: What challenges and developments await us in the realm of data privacy and security?

The digital age, with its boundless innovations, has woven a complex web of threats that evolve as swiftly as the technologies designed to counter them. Cybercriminals, wielding tools of deception and exploitation, are constantly finding new vulnerabilities to exploit. Imagine a shape-shifter, adept at slipping through the smallest of cracks, and you have a metaphor for the modern hacker. In this game of cat and mouse, the stakes are our personal and financial information, and the battleground is the entire digital world.

However, hope is far from lost. The future also holds remarkable promise in the form of advanced technologies designed to fortify our defenses. Blockchain technology, with its immutable ledger, offers a new paradigm for securing data transactions, creating a fortress that even the most skilled infiltrators struggle to breach. Artificial intelligence and machine learning algorithms are being trained to predict and neutralize threats before they can cause harm, acting as vigilant guardians of our digital sanctuaries.

Yet, technology alone cannot shoulder the burden of our digital safety. Public awareness stands as a beacon of hope, illuminating the path to a more secure future. It's a journey that begins with the individual, with the realization that knowledge is power. Have you ever paused to question the permissions you grant to the apps on your phone? Such contemplation is the first step in a larger movement towards digital literacy and empowerment.

Regulatory measures, too, are adapting to the shifting sands of the digital landscape. Legislators around the world are drafting laws that aim not just to react to breaches, but to prevent them. These laws envision a world where privacy is not a reactive measure, but a foundational principle of the digital age.

DATA DEMYSTIFIED: A BEGINNER'S GUIDE TO UNDERSTANDING THE WORLD THROUGH NUMBERS

Imagine a future where every new technology is born with privacy at its core, a future where the right to privacy is as inalienable as the right to freedom.

This vision of the future, however, is not a foregone conclusion. It is a possibility that requires effort, vigilance, and a shared commitment to the ideals of privacy and security. As digital citizens, we must remain ever watchful, ever ready to defend our rights in the face of evolving threats.

Consider this: when was the last time you reviewed the privacy settings on your social media accounts? Such actions, seemingly small in isolation, are the building blocks of a secure digital future. They are a testament to the power of the individual in shaping the digital landscape.

The future of data privacy and security is not written in the stars; it is forged by our choices, our actions, and our collective resolve. In this digital age, privacy and security are not just concerns of the individual but are a shared responsibility. It is a mantle we must all bear, a cause to which we must all contribute.

So, let us stride into the future with our eyes wide open, aware of the challenges but emboldened by the possibilities. Let us weave a tapestry of security and privacy that is as resilient as it is vibrant, creating a digital world where each of us can thrive, free from the shadows of exploitation and fear.

In the end, the future of data privacy and security is a narrative that we will write together. A story of triumph, of innovation, and of a shared commitment to safeguarding our digital destiny. Let this be our legacy: a world where privacy is protected, where security is assured, and where the digital age is a chapter in the story of humanity that we can all be proud of.

The journey does not end here. It is an ongoing voyage, a perpetual quest for balance in a world that teeters on the edge of the digital and the tangible. Stay informed, stay vigilant, and above all, stay proactive. The future is ours to shape. Let us do so with wisdom, with courage, and with an unwavering commitment to the ideals of privacy and security.

The digital age beckons. Let us answer the call.

Conclusion: Navigating the Data-Driven Future

Embarking on this journey through the mesmerizing universe of data, we've traversed landscapes rich with numbers, charts, and statistical models, each revealing its own story about the world we inhabit. It's akin to piecing together a vast puzzle, where every datum adds depth and dimension to the picture of reality. Reflecting on this odyssey, one cannot help but marvel at the insights gleaned from the myriad sections of this book. Data, as we've discovered, is not just a collection of numbers or facts. It's a beacon that illuminates the path to understanding complex phenomena, from the minutiae of daily life to the grand tapestry of global events.

Data literacy emerges not merely as a skill but as a critical lens through which to view the world. It empowers individuals to sift through the noise, discern patterns, and unearth truths hidden in plain sight. With this ability, asking the right questions becomes second nature, enabling informed decisions that resonate with personal and collective well-being. Indeed, to be data-literate is to hold a key to unlocking vast stores of knowledge, fostering a deeper connection with the world around us.

Yet, our quest for data literacy does not conclude with the final page of this book. Rather, it signals the commencement of a lifelong expedition into the realms of numbers, charts, and algorithms. The landscape of data is ever-changing, with new technologies, methodologies, and ethical considerations emerging at breakneck speed. How, then, can we continue to navigate this dynamic terrain?

The answer lies in an unwavering curiosity and a commitment to continuous learning. Engaging with online communities of data enthusiasts, attending workshops and seminars, and enrolling in courses are but a few avenues through which one can stay abreast of the latest developments. Websites, podcasts, and books dedicated to the art and science of data offer invaluable resources for those eager to deepen their understanding and refine their skills.

However, as we venture further into this data-driven future, a word of caution is warranted. With great power comes great responsibility. The ability to collect,

DATA DEMYSTIFIED: A BEGINNER'S GUIDE TO UNDERSTANDING THE WORLD THROUGH NUMBERS

analyze, and interpret data bestows upon us a duty to wield this power ethically and responsibly. We must advocate for practices that ensure transparency, fairness, and respect for privacy and human rights. In doing so, we contribute to a future where data serves as a force for good, enhancing lives and fostering a just society.

Resources for further learning abound, each offering a unique perspective on the evolving field of data science. Among these treasures, one might explore:

- "The Signal and the Noise" by Nate Silver, a compelling exploration of the art of prediction in a data-saturated world.

- Coursera and edX, platforms that offer a wealth of courses on data science, machine learning, and statistics, taught by experts from leading universities.

- The Data Science Podcast and Partially Derivative, podcasts that delve into the latest trends, technologies, and ethical dilemmas in the field of data science.

- Privacy International, a website dedicated to the protection of privacy rights in an increasingly data-driven society.

In closing, let us not view the conclusion of this book as an end but as a gateway to further exploration and discovery. The journey of data literacy is perpetual, marked by continuous learning and adaptation. As we navigate this ever-expanding universe of data, let us do so with a sense of purpose, curiosity, and responsibility. For in our hands lies the power to shape a future where data not only enlightens but elevates the human experience.

Remember, the story of data is the story of us all. It is a narrative that we write together, one data point at a time.

Did you love *Data Demystified: A Beginner's Guide to Understanding the World Through Numbers*? Then you should read *Leadership in the Age of Data: Harnessing Information for Strategic Advantage* by Ikwe Gideon!

In an era where data is the new currency, "Leadership in the Age of Data: Harnessing Information for Strategic Advantage" emerges as a seminal guide for leaders navigating the complexities of the digital landscape. This book marks a crucial paradigm shift, urging leaders to embrace data analytics not as a supplementary tool but as a cornerstone of strategic decision-making.

Through a meticulously crafted narrative, the book unveils the evolution of data-driven leadership, transitioning from the intuitive decision-making of the past to strategies enriched with data analytics. It arms leaders with the essential knowledge, skills, and mindset required to thrive in a data-centric world, placing a strong emphasis on data literacy, the ethical use of data, and strategic data utilization.

From the foundational aspects of understanding the varied data landscape, including structured, unstructured, and semi-structured data, to navigating the ethical considerations surrounding data usage, this book offers a comprehensive roadmap. It elucidates the qualities of data-savvy leaders—analytical mindset, visionary thinking, decisiveness, and the capacity to inspire data-driven teams—while also providing practical strategies for embedding data practices within organizations.

"Leadership in the Age of Data" delves into the mechanics of integrating data analytics into decision-making processes, overcoming biases, and aligning data strategy with organizational goals. It showcases success stories and case studies of companies and leaders who have innovated and driven their organizations forward through data-driven insights. Moreover, the book explores the burgeoning role of emerging technologies such as AI, machine learning, and IoT in shaping future leadership practices.

By fostering a culture of data-driven experimentation and cultivating teams equipped with diverse data skills, the book serves as a beacon for leaders aspiring to drive transformation in their organizations. It emphasizes the transformative power of data, encouraging leaders to leverage information for a competitive edge in the rapidly evolving business environment.

Concluding with a forward-looking perspective, "Leadership in the Age of Data" addresses emerging trends, the imperative for continuous learning, and the need for ethical AI practices. It synthesizes key strategies, lessons learned, and best practices for successful data-driven leadership, issuing a compelling call to action for leaders to embrace the data revolution for organizational success.

"Leadership in the Age of Data: Harnessing Information for Strategic Advantage" is not just a book; it's a journey into the heart of modern leadership, offering a glimpse into the future of organizational success in the age of data.

About the Author

With over eighteen years of progressive experience in data analysis, revenue assurance, business intelligence, risk management, and a profound understanding of Azure cloud services, Ikwe Gideon stands as a beacon of leadership in the telecom and technology sectors. His extensive background encompasses pivotal roles where he has driven data-driven strategies, managed intricate analytics projects, and spearheaded initiatives that significantly impacted operational efficiency and revenue growth.

Ikwe's career is marked by notable achievements, such as developing over 120 monitoring LTE network KPIs use by major telecom for analytics and strategic decision-making. His proactive fraud detection strategies safeguarded companies from potential losses amounting to hundreds of millions. By steering the transition of prepaid revenue reporting to align with International Financial Reporting Standards (IFRS) at Mobile Communication Company of Iran (MCCI), he showcased his commitment to accuracy and transparency in financial reporting.

As a seasoned Business Intelligence and Data Analyst, Ikwe possesses a deep skill set in software and financial management tools, including proficiency in Oracle PL/SQL, Microsoft SQL Navigator, ETL tools like Oracle Data Integrator, and data visualization using Qlikview, Tableau, and Power BI. His strategic approach to data architecture, coupled with his expertise in predictive analytics and big data ecosystems, enables him to devise solutions that drive competitive advantage.

His educational background in Mathematics/Statistics, complemented by professional certifications such as ACA and CFA (Level III candidate), and technical certifications in Microsoft Azure and Power BI, underscores his robust analytical foundation and cloud computing prowess.

Ikwe Gideon is dedicated to leveraging his vast experience and Azure expertise to assist telecom companies in navigating the complexities of digital transformation. By implementing cutting-edge Azure solutions for revenue assurance, fraud detection, and business intelligence, he aims to empower telecom companies to optimize their operations, enhance decision-making, and achieve sustainable growth in the ever-evolving digital landscape.

www.ingramcontent.com/pod-product-compliance
Lightning Source LLC
Chambersburg PA
CBHW052157220526
45471CB00004B/1703